Whitefield Public Library
Whitefield, N

S0-AFR-416

Fodor's 99
Pocket
Washington,
D.C.

DISCARDED

917.7
F

Excerpted from *Fodor's Washington, D.C. 99*

Fodor's Travel Publications, Inc.
New York • Toronto • London • Sydney • Auckland
www.fodors.com

Fodor's Pocket Washington, D.C.

EDITOR: Laura M. Kidder and Stephanie J. Adler

Editorial Contributors: Holly Bass, Anna Borgman, David Brown, Neil Chesanow, Michael Dolan, Thomas Head, John F. Kelly, Deborah Papier, Betty Ross, Helayne Schiff, M. T. Schwartzman (Gold Guide editor), Bruce Walker, CiCi Williamson, Stephen Wolf, Jan Ziegler

Editorial Production: Melissa Klurman

Maps: David Lindroth, *cartographer*; Steven Amsterdam and Robert Blake, *map editors*

Design: Fabrizio La Rocca, *creative director*; Guido Caroti, *associate art director*; Lyndell Brookhouse-Gil, *cover design*; Jolie Novak, *photo editor*

Production/Manufacturing: Mike Costa

Cover Photograph: James Lemass

Copyright

Copyright © 1998 by Fodor's Travel Publications, Inc.

Fodor's is a registered trademark of Fodor's Travel Publications, Inc.

All rights reserved under International and Pan-American Copyright Conventions. Published in the United States by Fodor's Travel Publications, Inc., a subsidiary of Random House, Inc., New York, and simultaneously in Canada by Random House of Canada Limited, Toronto. Distributed by Random House, Inc., New York.

No maps, illustrations, or other portions of this book may be reproduced in any form without written permission from the publisher.

ISBN 0–679–00176–X

Special Sales

Fodor's Travel Publications are available at special discounts for bulk purchases for sales promotions or premiums. Special editions, including personalized covers, excerpts of existing guides, and corporate imprints, can be created in large quantities for special needs. For more information, contact your local bookseller or write to Special Markets, Fodor's Travel Publications, 201 East 50th Street, New York, NY 10022. Inquiries from Canada should be directed to your local Canadian bookseller or sent to Random House of Canada, Ltd., Marketing Department, 2775 Matheson Blvd. E, Mississauga, Ontario, L4W 4P7. Inquiries from the United Kingdom should be sent to Fodor's Travel Publications, 20 Vauxhall Bridge Road, London SW1V 2SA.

PRINTED IN THE UNITED STATES OF AMERICA

10 9 8 7 6 5 4 3 2 1

CONTENTS

Maps

ON THE ROAD WITH FODOR'S

WHEN I PLAN A VA-
CATION, the first
thing I do is cast
around among my friends and col-
leagues to find someone who's
just been where I'm going. That's
because there's no substitute for a
recommendation from a good
friend who knows your tastes,
your budget, and your circum-
stances, someone who's just been
there. Unfortunately, such friends
are few and far between. So it's
nice to know that there's *Fodor's
Pocket Washington, D.C. '99.*

It has been written and assiduously
updated by the kind of people you
would hit up for travel tips if you
knew them. In these pages, they
don't send you chasing down every
sight in Washington, but have instead selected the best ones, the
ones that are worthy of your time
and money.

About Our Writers

Our success in achieving our goals
is a credit to the hard work of our
extraordinary writers.

Holly Bass, who updated the Shopping and Nightlife and the Arts
chapters, is a performer and a
writer. Dining chapter updater
Thomas Head is the executive wine
and food editor at *The Washing-*
tonian magazine. **Bruce Walker,** a
DC–area resident for most of his
life, has been with the *Washington
Post* since 1981. He updated the
Exploring and Sports and Outdoor
Activities chapters. **CiCi Williamson,**
who revised the Lodging chapter,
has been a food and travel writer
and syndicated newspaper colum-
nist for almost two decades.

Connections

We're pleased that the American Society of Travel Agents continues to
endorse Fodor's as its guidebook of
choice. ASTA is the world's largest
and most influential travel trade
association, operating in more than
170 countries, with 27,000 members pledged to adhere to a strict
code of ethics reflecting the society's
motto, "Integrity in Travel." ASTA
shares Fodor's devotion to providing smart, honest travel information and advice to travelers, and
we've long recommended that our
readers—even those who have
guidebooks and traveling friends—
consult ASTA member agents for
the experience and professional-
ism they bring to your vacation
planning.

On Fodor's Web site
(www.fodors.com), check out the
new Resource Center, an online
companion to the Essential Infor-

mation section of this book, complete with useful hot links to related sites. In our forums, you can also get lively advice from other travelers and more great tips from Fodor's experts worldwide.

How to Use This Book

Organization

Up front is the **Essential Information,** an easy-to-use section arranged alphabetically by topic. Under each listing you'll find tips and information that will help you accomplish what you need to in Washington, DC. You'll also find addresses and telephone numbers of organizations and companies that offer destination-related services and detailed information and publications.

The first chapter in the guide, **Destination: Washington, DC,** aims to get you in the mood for your trip. Quick Tours lays out a selection of half-day itineraries that will help you make the most of your time in Washington, DC.

The **Exploring Washington, DC,** chapter is divided into nine neighborhoods; each lists sights alphabetically and includes a map. The remaining chapters are arranged in alphabetical order by subject— **Dining, Lodging, Nightlife and the Arts,** and **Shopping.**

Icons and Symbols

★   Our special recommendations
✕   Restaurant

🏠   Lodging establishment
🐥   Good for kids (rubber duckie)
☞   Sends you to another section of the guide for more information
✉   Address
☎   Telephone number
🕐   Opening and closing times
🎟   Admission prices (prices we give apply to adults)

Numbers in black circles (e.g., ❸) that appear on the maps and in the margins correspond to one another.

Dining and Lodging

The restaurants and lodgings we list are the cream of the crop in each price range. Price categories are as follows:

For restaurants:

CATEGORY	COST*
$$$$	over $35
$$$	$26–$35
$$	$15–$25
$	under $15

*per person for a three-course meal, excluding drinks, service, and sales tax (10% in DC, 4.5%–9% in VA).

For hotels:

CATEGORY	COST*
$$$$	over $190
$$$	$145–$190
$$	$100–$145
$	under $100

*All prices are for a standard double room, excluding room tax (13% in DC, and 6.5 to 9.75% in VA) and $1.50 per night occupancy tax in DC.

Hotel Facilities

We always list the facilities that are available—but we don't specify whether you'll be charged extra to use them: When pricing accommodations, always ask what's included. In addition, assume that all rooms have private baths unless noted otherwise.

Assume that hotels operate on the **European Plan** (EP, with no meals) unless we note that they use the **American Plan** (AP, with all meals), the **Breakfast Plan** (BP, with full breakfast), the **Continental Plan** (CP, with Continental breakfast), or the **Modified American Plan** (MAP, with breakfast and dinner).

Restaurant Reservations and Dress Codes

Reservations are always a good idea; we mention them only when they're essential or are not accepted. Unless otherwise noted, the restaurants listed are open daily for lunch and dinner. We mention dress only when men are required to wear a jacket or a jacket and tie.

Credit Cards

The following abbreviations are used: **AE,** American Express; **D,** Discover; **DC,** Diners Club; **MC,** MasterCard; and **V,** Visa.

Don't Forget to Write

You can use this book in the confidence that all prices and opening times are based on information supplied to us at press time; Fodor's cannot accept responsibility for any errors. Time inevitably brings changes, so always confirm information when it matters—especially if you're making a detour to visit a specific place.

Were the restaurants we recommended as described? Did our hotel picks exceed your expectations? Did you find a museum we recommended a waste of time? Keeping a travel guide fresh and up-to-date is a big job, and we welcome your feedback, positive *and* negative. If you have complaints, we'll look into them and revise our entries when the facts warrant it. If you've discovered a special place that we haven't included, we'll pass the information along to our correspondents and have them check it out. So send us your thoughts via E-mail at editors@fodors.com (specifying the name of the book on the subject line) or on paper in care of the Washington, D.C., editor at Fodor's, 201 East 50th Street, New York, New York 10022. In the meantime, have a wonderful trip!

Karen Cure
Editorial Director

Washington, DC, Area

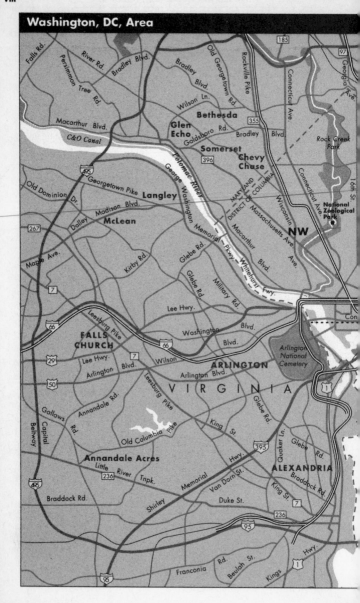

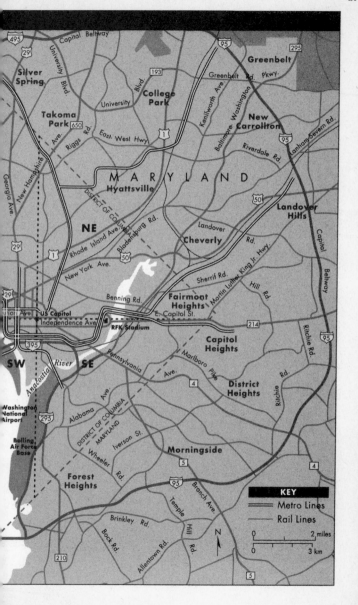

495
29

Capital Beltway

Silver Spring

University Blvd

193

95

295

Greenbelt

Greenbelt Rd. Pkwy.

University Blvd

College Park

Takoma Park

650

East- West Hwy.

Riggs Rd.

1

Kenilworth Ave.

Baltimore Washington

New Carrollton

Riverdale Rd.

95

Lanham-Severn Rd.

M A R Y L A N D

Hyattsville

50

Landover

Landover Hills

Georgia Ave.

New Hampshire

DISTRICT OF COLUMBIA

NE

Rhode Island Ave.

Bladensburg Rd.

29

1

50

New York Ave.

Cheverly

Rd.

Martin Luther King Jr. Hwy.

Hill Rd.

Capital Beltway

95

Benning Rd.

Sherrif Rd.

Fairmont Heights

E. Capitol St.

29

US Capitol

Independence Ave.

RFK Stadium

214

Ritchie Rd.

SW

395

River

SE

Anacostia

Pennsylvania

Capitol Heights

Marlboro Pike

4

District Heights

Ritchie

Rd.

95

Washington National Airport

295

Alabama Ave.

DISTRICT OF COLUMBIA

MARYLAND

Iverson St.

Ave.

Morningside

5

Bolling Air Force Base

Wheeler Rd.

4

Forest Heights

95

Branch Ave.

Brinkley Rd.

Temple Hill Rd.

KEY
≡≡≡ Metro Lines
— Rail Lines

N

Bock Rd.

Allentown Rd.

210

5

0   2 miles

0   3 km

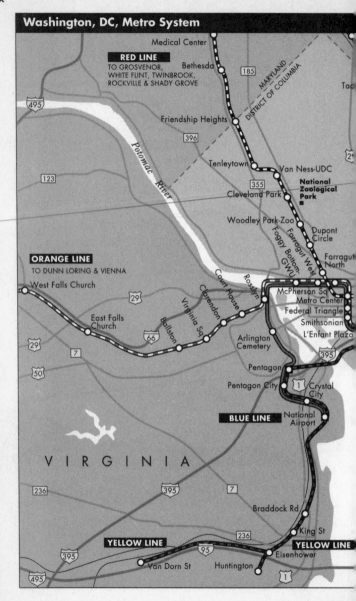

Washington, DC, Metro System

x

RED LINE
TO GROSVENOR,
WHITE FLINT, TWINBROOK,
ROCKVILLE & SHADY GROVE

Medical Center

Bethesda

MARYLAND
DISTRICT OF COLUMBIA

185

Tac

Friendship Heights

396

2

Tenleytown

Van Ness-UDC

355

**National
Zoological
Park**

Cleveland Park

Woodley Park-Zoo

Dupont
Circle

Farragut
North

ORANGE LINE
TO DUNN LORING & VIENNA

West Falls Church

Rosslyn

Court House

Clarendon

Virginia Sq

Ballston

East Falls
Church

McPherson Sq

Metro Center

Federal Triangle

Smithsonian

L'Enfant Plaza

Arlington
Cemetery

Pentagon

Pentagon City

Crystal
City

BLUE LINE

National
Airport

V I R G I N I A

Braddock Rd

King St

YELLOW LINE

YELLOW LINE

Eisenhower

Van Dorn St

Huntington

Potomac River

Farragut West

Foggy Bottom-
GWU

495

123

29

66

7

50

236

395

7

236

95

395

495

1

1

1

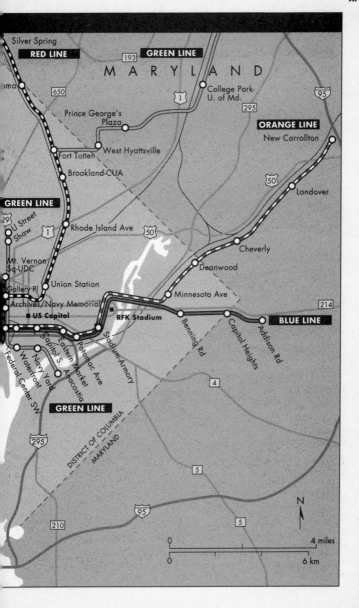

ESSENTIAL INFORMATION

Basic Information on Traveling in Washington, DC, Savvy Tips to Make Your Trip a Breeze, and Companies and Organizations to Contact

AIR TRAVEL

CARRIERS

➤ MAJOR AIRLINES: **Air Canada** (☎ 800/776–3000) to Ronald Reagan National, Dulles, BWI. **America West** (☎ 800/235–9292) to Ronald Reagan National, Dulles, and BWI. **American** (☎ 800/433–7300) to Ronald Reagan National, Dulles, and BWI. **Continental** (☎ 800/525–0280) to Ronald Reagan National, Dulles, and BWI. **Delta** (☎ 800/221–1212) to Ronald Reagan National, Dulles, and BWI. **Northwest** (☎ 800/225–2525) to Ronald Reagan National, Dulles, and BWI. **TWA** (☎ 800/221–2000) to Ronald Reagan National, Dulles, and BWI. **United** (☎ 800/241–6522) to Ronald Reagan National, Dulles, and BWI. **US Airways** (☎ 800/428–4322) to Ronald Reagan National, Dulles, and BWI.

➤ SMALLER AIRLINES: **Air Tram** (☎ 800/VALUJET) to Dulles. **Midway** (☎ 800/446–4392) to Ronald Reagan National and BWI. **Midwest Express** (☎ 800/452–2022) to Ronald Reagan National. **Southwest** (☎ 800/435–9792) to BWI.

FLYING TIMES

A flight to DC from New York takes a little less than an hour. It's about 1½ hours from Chicago, three hours from Denver, and five hours from San Francisco. Those flying from London can expect a trip of about six hours.

AIRPORTS & TRANSFERS

AIRPORTS

The major gateways to DC include **Ronald Reagan National Airport**, in Virginia, 4 mi south of downtown Washington; **Dulles International Airport**, 26 mi west of Washington; and **Baltimore-Washington International (BWI) Airport**, in Maryland, about 25 mi northeast of Washington.

➤ AIRPORT INFORMATION: **Ronald Reagan National Airport** (☎ 703/417–8000). **Dulles International Airport** (☎ 703/572–2700). **Baltimore-Washington International (BWI) Airport** (☎ 410/859–7100).

TRANSFERS BY BUS

Dulles airport is served every half hour (hourly on weekends) by **Washington Flyer**. The ride from Dulles to downtown takes 45 minutes and costs $16 ($26 round-trip). The bus takes you to 1517 K Street NW, where you can board a free shuttle bus that serves downtown hotels. Fares may be paid in cash or with Visa or MasterCard; children under age six ride free. National and BWI airports are served by **SuperShuttle**. Buses leave National and BWI every half hour for 1517 K Street NW. The 20-minute ride from National costs $8 ($14 round-trip); the 65-minute ride from BWI costs $21 ($31 round-trip); drivers accept major credit cards in addition to cash.

➤ BUS INFORMATION: **Washington Flyer** (☎ 703/685–1400). **Super-Shuttle** (☎ 800/258–3826).

TRANSFERS BY LIMOUSINE

Call at least a day ahead and **Destination Limo** will have a limousine waiting for you at the airport. The ride downtown from National, BWI, or Dulles is $86.25, including tip.

➤ LIMOUSINE INFORMATION: **Destination Limo** (☎ 703/863–5670).

TRANSFERS BY SUBWAY

If you are coming into National Airport, have little to carry, and are staying at a hotel near a subway stop, it makes sense to take the Metro downtown. The station is within walking distance of the baggage claim area, but a free airport shuttle stops outside each terminal and brings you to the National Airport station. The Metro ride downtown takes about

20 minutes and costs either $1.10 or $1.40, depending on the time of day.

TRANSFERS BY TAXI

Expect to pay about $13 to get from National Airport to downtown, $45 from Dulles, and $50 from BWI. Unscrupulous cabbies prey on out-of-towners, so if the fare strikes you as astronomical, get the driver's name and cab number and threaten to call the **D.C. Taxicab Commission**. A $1.25 airport surcharge is added to the total at National.

➤ TAXI INFORMATION: **D.C. Taxicab Commission** (☎ 202/645–6018).

TRANSFERS BY TRAIN

Free shuttle buses carry passengers between airline terminals and the train station at BWI Airport. **Amtrak** and **Maryland Rail Commuter Service** trains run between BWI and Washington's Union Station from around 6 AM to midnight. The cost of the 40-minute ride is $13–$22 on an Amtrak train, $5 on a MARC train (weekdays only).

➤ TRAIN INFORMATION: **Amtrak** (☎ 800/872–7245). **Maryland Rail Commuter Service** (MARC, ☎ 800/325–7245).

BUS TRAVEL

Washington is a major terminal for **Greyhound Bus Lines**. The company also has stations in nearby Silver Spring, Maryland,

and in Arlington and Springfield, Virginia.

WMATA's red, white, and blue Metrobuses crisscross the city and nearby suburbs, with some routes running 24 hours. All bus rides within the District are $1.10. Free transfers, good for 1½ to two hours, are available on buses and in Metro stations. Bus-to-bus transfers are accepted at designated Metrobus transfer points. Rail-to-bus transfers must be picked up before boarding the train. There may be a transfer charge when boarding the bus. There are no bus-to-rail transfers.

➤ INFORMATION: **Greyhound Bus Lines** (⌧ 1005 1st St. NE, ☎ 202/289–5160 or 800/231–2222). **Washington Metropolitan Area Transit Authority** (WMATA, ☎ 202/637–7000 or 202/638–3780 TDD); open weekdays 6 AM–10:30 PM and weekends 8 AM–10:30 PM. Call for schedule and route information.

BUSINESS HOURS

MUSEUMS

Museums are usually open daily 10–5:30; some have later hours on Thursday. Many private museums are closed Monday or Tuesday, and some museums in government buildings are closed weekends. The Smithsonian often sets extended spring and summer hours for some of its museums.

SHOPS

Stores are generally open Monday–Saturday 10–7 (or 8). Some have extended hours on Thursday and many open Sunday anywhere from 10 to noon and close at 5 or 6.

CAR RENTAL

In Washington, DC, you must be 21 to rent a car, and rates may be higher if you're under 25. Rates in Washington begin at $38 a day and $139 a week for an economy car with air-conditioning, an automatic transmission, and unlimited mileage. This does not include tax on car rentals, which is 8%.

➤ MAJOR AGENCIES: **Alamo** (☎ 800/327–9633, 0800/272–2000 in the U.K.). **Avis** (☎ 800/331–1212, 800/879–2847 in Canada). **Budget** (☎ 800/527–0700, 0800/181181 in the U.K.). **Dollar** (☎ 800/800–4000; 0990/565656 in the U.K., where it is known as Eurodollar). **Hertz** (☎ 800/654–3131, 800/263–0600 in Canada, 0345/555888 in the U.K.). **National InterRent** (☎ 800/227–7368; 0345/222525 in the U.K., where it is known as Europcar InterRent).

CAR TRAVEL

A car can be a drawback in Washington. Traffic is horrendous, especially at rush hours, and **driving is often confusing,** with many lanes and some entire streets changing direction suddenly at certain times of day. Radar detectors are illegal in Washington, DC, and Virginia.

LAY OF THE LAND

I–95 skirts DC as part of the Beltway, the six- to eight-lane highway that encircles the city. The eastern half of the Beltway is labeled both I–95 and I–495; the western half is just I–495. If you are coming from the south, take I–95 to I–395 and cross the 14th Street Bridge to 14th Street in the District. From the north, stay on I–95 south before heading west on Route 50, the John Hanson Highway, which turns into New York Avenue.

I–66 approaches the city from the southwest, but you may not be able to use it during weekday rush hours, when high-occupancy vehicle (HOV) restrictions apply: Cars must carry at least two people from 6:30 AM to 9 AM traveling eastbound inside the Beltway (I–495) and 4 PM to 6:30 PM traveling westbound. If you're traveling at off-peak hours or have enough people in your car to satisfy the rules, you can get downtown by taking I–66 across the Theodore Roosevelt Bridge to Constitution Avenue.

I–270 approaches Washington from the northwest before hitting I–495. To get downtown, take I–495 east to Connecticut Avenue south, toward Chevy Chase.

PARKING

Parking in Washington is an adventure; the **police are quick to tow** away or immobilize with a "boot" any vehicle parked illegally. (If you find you've been towed from a city street, call ☎ 202/727–5000.) Since the city's most popular sights are within a short walk of a Metro station anyway, **it's best to leave your car at the hotel.** Touring by car is a good idea only if you're considering visiting sights in Maryland or Virginia.

Most of the outlying, suburban Metro stations have parking lots, though these fill quickly with city-bound commuters. If you plan to park in one of these lots, arrive early, armed with lots of quarters. Private **parking lots downtown are expensive,** charging as much as $4 an hour and $13 a day. There's free, two-hour parking around the Mall on Jefferson Drive and Madison Drive, though these spots are always filled. You can park free—in some spots all day—in parking areas off of Ohio Drive near the Jefferson Memorial and south of the Lincoln Memorial on Ohio Drive and West Basin Drive in West Potomac Park.

CUSTOMS & DUTIES

Keep receipts for all of your purchases. Upon reentering the country, **be ready to show customs officials what you've bought.** If you feel a duty is incorrect, appeal the assessment. If you object to the way your clearance was handled, get the inspector's badge number. In either case, ask to see a supervisor, then write to the appropriate authorities, beginning with the port director at your point of entry.

IN CANADA

Canadian residents who have been out of Canada for at least seven days may bring in C$500 worth of goods duty-free. If you've been away less than seven days but more than 48 hours, the duty-free allowance drops to C$200; if your trip lasts 24–48 hours, the allowance is C$50. You may send an unlimited number of gifts worth up to C$60 each duty-free to Canada. Label the package UN-SOLICITED GIFT—VALUE UNDER $60. Alcohol and tobacco are excluded.

➤ INFORMATION: **Revenue Canada** (✉ 2265 St. Laurent Blvd. S, Ottawa, Ontario K1G 4K3, ☎ 613/993–0534, 800/461–9999 in Canada).

IN THE U.K.

From the United States, you may import, duty-free, 200 cigarettes or 50 cigars; 1 liter of spirits or 2 liters of fortified or sparkling wine or liqueurs; 2 liters of still table wine; 60 milliliters of perfume; 250 milliliters of toilet water; plus £136 worth of other goods, including gifts and souvenirs.

➤ INFORMATION: **HM Customs and Excise** (✉ Dorset House, Stamford St., London SE1 9NG, ☎ 0171/202–4227).

DISABILITIES & ACCESSIBILITY

ACCESS IN WASHINGTON

The Metro has excellent facilities for visitors with vision and hearing impairments or mobility problems. Virtually all streets have wide, level sidewalks with curb cuts, though in Georgetown the brick-paved terrain can be bumpy. Most museums and monuments are accessible to visitors using wheelchairs.

➤ INFORMATION: The **Washington Convention andVisitors Association** (☎ 202/789–7000) has a four-page publication full of tips and contacts. The **Washington MTA** (☎ 202/635–6434) publishes a metro and bus system guide. The **Smithsonian** (202/357–1729 or 202/357–2700 TDD) publishes an access guide to all its museums.

EMERGENCIES

➤ DOCTORS & DENTISTS: **1-800-DOCTORS** (☎ 800/362–8677) is a referral service that locates doctors, dentists, and urgent-care clinics in the greater Washington area. The hospital closest to downtown is **George Washington University Hospital** (✉ 901 23rd St. NW, ☎ 202/994–3211 emergencies only). The **D.C. Dental Society** (☎ 202/547–7615) operates a referral line weekdays 8–4.

➤ EMERGENCIES: Dial 911 for police, fire, or ambulance in an emergency.

➤ HOSPITALS: **Children's National Medical Center** (⊠ 111 Michigan Ave. NW, ☎ 202/884–5000). **Georgetown University Medical Center** (⊠ 3800 Reservoir Rd., ☎ 202/342–2400). **Washington Hospital Center** (⊠ 110 Irving St. NW, ☎ 202/877–7000).

➤ 24-HOUR PHARMACIES: **CVS Pharmacy** operates 24-hour pharmacies at 14th Street and Thomas Circle NW (☎ 202/628–0720) and at 7 Dupont Circle NW (☎ 202/785–1466).

HOLIDAYS

Major national holidays include: New Year's Day (Jan. 1); Martin Luther King, Jr., Day (3rd Mon. in Jan.); President's Day (3rd Mon. in Feb.); Memorial Day (last Mon. in May); Independence Day (July 4); Labor Day (1st Mon. in Sept.); Thanksgiving Day (4th Thurs. in Nov.); Christmas Eve and Day (Dec. 24–25); and New Year's Eve (Dec. 31).

MONEY

CREDIT & DEBIT CARDS

A credit card allows you to delay payment and gives you certain rights as a consumer. A debit card, also known as a check card, deducts funds directly from your checking account and helps you stay within your budget. Note that although you can always *pay* for a rental car with a debit card, some agencies won't allow you to *reserve* a car with one. Otherwise, the two types of plastic are virtually the same. Both will get you cash advances at ATMs worldwide if your card is properly programmed with your personal identification number (PIN).

➤ ATM LOCATIONS: **Cirrus** (☎ 800/424–7787). **Plus** (☎ 800/843–7587) for locations in the U.S. and Canada, or visit your local bank.

NATIONAL MONUMENTS

Look into discount passes to **save money on monument and battlefield entrance fees.** The Golden Eagle Pass ($50) gets you and your companions free admission to all parks for one year. (Camping and parking are extra). Both the Golden Age Passport ($10), for those 62 and older, and the Golden Access Passport (free), for travelers with disabilities, entitle holders to free entry to all national parks, plus 50% off fees for the use of many park facilities and services. You must show proof of age and of U.S. citizenship or permanent residency (such as a U.S. passport, driver's license, or birth certificate) and, if requesting Golden Access, proof of disability. All three passes are available at all national park entrances where entrance fees are charged. Golden Eagle and Golden Access passes are also available by mail.

➤ PASSES BY MAIL: **National Park Service** (⊠ National Capitol Area Office, 1100 Ohio Dr. SW, Washington, DC 20242).

PASSPORTS & VISAS

When traveling internationally, **carry a passport even if you don't need one** (it's always the best form of ID), and make **two photocopies of the data page** (one for someone at home and another for you, carried separately from your passport). If you lose your passport, promptly call the nearest embassy or consulate and the local police.

CANADIANS

A passport is not required to enter the United States.

U.K. CITIZENS

British citizens need a valid passport to enter the United States. If you are staying for fewer than 90 days on vacation, with a return or onward ticket, you probably will not need a visa. However, you will need to fill out the Visa Waiver Form, 1-94W, supplied by the airline.

➤ U.K. CITIZENS: **U.S. Embassy Visa Information Line** (☎ 01891/200–290; calls cost 49p per minute, 39p per minute cheap rate), for U.S. visa information. **U.S. Embassy Visa Branch** (⊠ 5 Upper Grosvenor St., London W1A 2JB), for U.S. visa information; send a self-addressed, stamped envelope. Write the U.S.

Consulate General (⊠ Queen's House, Queen St., Belfast BTI 6EO) if you live in Northern Ireland.

SIGHT-SEEING TOURS

BICYCLE TOURS

Bike the Sites, Inc. (☎ 202/966–8662) leads four tours geared to the occasional exerciser and will customize tours as well. Bicycles (21-speed Trek Hybrids), helmets, and water bottles are included. Licensed guides take groups on tours that range from one hour to a full day; prices are $25–$65.

BOAT TOURS

D.C. Ducks (☎ 202/832–9800) offers 90-minute tours in their converted World War II amphibious vehicles. After an hour-long road tour of prominent sights, the tour moves from land to water, as the vehicle is piloted into the waters of the Potomac for a 30-minute boat's-eye view of the city.

BUS TOURS

All About Town, Inc. (☎ 202/393–3696) has half-day, all-day, two-day, and twilight bus tours that drive by some sights and stop at others. An all-day tour costs $34.

PERSONAL GUIDES

Personal tour services include **Guide Service of Washington** (☎ 202/628–2842) and **A Tour de Force** (☎ 703/525–2948).

WALKING TOURS

The Black History National Recreation Trail links a group of sights within historic neighborhoods illustrating aspects of African-American history in Washington, from slavery days to the New Deal. A brochure outlining the trail is available from the **National Park Service** (☎ 202/619–7222). The **National Building Museum** (☎ 202/272–2448) sponsors several tours led by architectural historians. The **Smithsonian Resident Associate Program** (☎ 202/357–3030) routinely offers guided walks and bus tours of neighborhoods in Washington and communities outside the city.

SUBWAY TRAVEL

The WMATA provides bus and subway service in the District and in the Maryland and Virginia suburbs. The Metro, opened in 1976, is one of the country's cleanest and safest subway systems. Trains run weekdays 5:30 AM–midnight, weekends 8 AM–midnight. During the weekday rush hours (5:30–9:30 AM and 3–8 PM), trains come along every six minutes. At other times and on weekends and holidays, trains run about every 12–15 minutes. The base fare is $1.10; the actual price you pay depends on the time of day and the distance traveled. Children under age five ride free when accompanied by a paying passenger, but there is a maximum of two children per paying adult.

Buy your ticket at the Farecard machines; they accept coins and crisp $1, $5, $10, or $20 bills. The Farecard should be inserted into the turnstile to enter the platform. Make sure you **hang onto the card**—you'll need it to exit at your destination.

➤ INFORMATION: **Washington Metropolitan Area Transit Authority** (WMATA; ☎ 202/637–7000 or 202/638–3780 TDD); open weekdays 6 AM–10:30 PM, weekends 8 AM–10:30 PM.

DISCOUNT PASSES

For $5 you can **buy a pass that allows unlimited trips for one day.** It's good all day on weekends, on holidays, and after 9:30 AM on weekdays. Passes are available at Metro Sales Outlets and at many hotels, banks, and Safeway and Giant grocery stores.

TAXIS

Taxis in the District are not metered; they operate instead on a curious zone system. **Before you set off, ask your cab driver how much the fare will be.** The basic single rate for traveling within one zone is $3.20. There is an extra $1.25 charge for each additional passenger and a $1 surcharge during the 4–6:30 PM rush hour. Bulky suitcases are charged at a higher rate, and a $1.50 surcharge is tacked on when you phone for a cab. Maryland and Virginia taxis are metered but are not allowed to take passengers between points in DC.

TELEPHONES

The country code for the United States is 1. Competitive long-distance carriers make calling within the United States relatively convenient and let you avoid hotel surcharges. By dialing an 800 number, you can get connected to the long-distance company of your choice.

➤ LONG-DISTANCE CARRIERS: **AT&T** (☎ 800/225–5288). **MCI** (☎ 800/888–8000). **Sprint** (☎ 800/366–2255).

TRAIN TRAVEL

More than 80 trains a day arrive at Washington, DC's **Union Station** on Capitol Hill (⊠ 50 Massachusetts Ave. NE, ☎ 202/484–7540 or 800/872–7245).

VISITOR INFORMATION

➤ CITYWIDE INFORMATION: **Washington, D.C. Convention and Visitors Association** (⊠ 1212 New York Ave. NW, Suite 600, Washington, DC 20005, ☎ 202/789–7000, www.washington.org). **D.C. Committee to Promote Washington** (⊠ 1212 New York Ave. NW, Ste. 200, Washington, DC 20005, ☎ 202/724–5644 or 800/422–8644).

➤ EVENTS AND ATTRACTIONS: **White House Visitor Center** (⊠ Baldridge Hall, Dept. of Commerce, 1450 Pennsylvania Ave. NW, ☎ 202/208–1631, www.whitehouse.gov). **Dial-A-Park** (☎ 202/619–7275). **Dial-A-Museum** (☎ 202/357–2020).

➤ NATIONAL PARKS: **National Park Service** (⊠ Office of Public Affairs, National Capital Region, 1100 Ohio Dr. SW, Washington, DC 20242, ☎ 202/619–7222, www.nps.gov).

WHEN TO GO

Washington has **two delightful seasons: spring and autumn.** In spring, the city's ornamental fruit trees are budding, and its many gardens are in bloom. By autumn, most of the summer crowds have left and you can enjoy the sights in peace. Summers can be uncomfortably hot and humid. Winter weather is often bitter, with a handful of modest snowstorms that somehow bring this Southern city to a standstill. If you're interested in government, visit when Congress is in session. When lawmakers break for recess (at Christmas, Easter, July 4, and other holiday periods), the city seems a little less vibrant.

CLIMATE

What follows are the average daily maximum and minimum temperatures for Washington.

Jan.	47F	8C	May	76F	24C	Sept.	79F	26C
	34	− 1		58	14		61	16
Feb.	47F	8C	June	85F	29C	Oct.	70F	21C
	31	− 1		65	18		52	11
Mar.	56F	13C	July	88F	31C	Nov.	56F	13C
	38	3		70	21		41	5
Apr.	67F	19C	Aug.	86F	30C	Dec.	47F	8C
	47	8		68	20		32	0

➤ FORECASTS: **Weather Channel Connection** (☎ 900/932–8437), *95¢* per minute from a Touch-Tone phone.

1 Destination: Washington, DC

AMERICA'S HOMETOWN

TO A SURPRISING DEGREE, life in Washington isn't that different from life elsewhere in the country. People are born here, grow up here, get jobs here—by no means invariably with the federal government—and go on to have children, who repeat the cycle. Very often, they live out their lives without ever testifying before Congress, being indicted for influence peddling, or attending a state dinner at the White House.

Which is not to say that the federal government doesn't cast a long shadow over the city. Among Washington's 543,000 inhabitants are an awful lot of lawyers, journalists, and people who include the word "policy" in their job titles. It's just that DC is much more of a hometown than most visitors realize.

Just a few blocks away from the monuments and museums on the Mall are residential and business districts whose scale is very human. The houses are a crazy quilt of architectural styles, kept in linear formation by rows of lush trees. On the commercial streets, bookstores and ethnic groceries abound.

Redevelopment has left its mark. Fourteenth Street was once the capital's red-light district. The city was determined to clean up the strip, and to everyone's surprise it succeeded. Nor is much left of the tacky commercial district around 9th and F streets. Washington's original downtown, it deteriorated when the city's center shifted to the west, to the "new" downtown of Connecticut Avenue and K Street. But the "old" downtown is being rejuvenated. The department stores that once drew crowds with their window displays have been renovated; there are new hotels and office buildings; and as the construction dust clears, the area is looking good.

Many people who come here are worried about crime. Crime is certainly a major problem, as it is in other big cities, but Washington isn't nearly as dangerous as its well-publicized homicide rate might lead you to believe. Most visitors have relatively little to fear. Unless you go seeking out the drug markets, there isn't much chance you'll get caught in the cross fire of rival gangs. Crimes against property are more widespread, but still far from ubiquitous. Unlike New York, Washington is not full of expert pickpockets, nor is it plagued by gold-chain snatchers.

The city's Metro is generally safe, even at night. However, if you have to walk from your stop in a neighborhood that isn't well lit and trafficked, you probably should invest in a taxi. Of course, even exercising normal prudence, it's still possible that you will have an encounter with someone who believes that what's yours ought to be his or hers. If that happens, don't argue.

Your attachment to the contents of your wallet is certain to be tested in another way, however. Panhandlers are now a fixture of the cityscape, and there's no avoiding their importunities. How you respond to them is a matter on which only your conscience can advise you. Wealth and poverty have always coexisted in America's hometown; but poverty is now omnipresent, wearing a very human face.

— By Deborah Papier

A native of Washington, Deborah Papier is an editor and writer for numerous newspapers and magazines.

QUICK TOURS

If you're here for just a short period you need to plan carefully so as to make the most of your time in Washington, DC. The following itineraries outline major sights throughout the city, and will help you structure your visit efficiently. Each is intended to take about four hours—a perfect way to fill a free morning or afternoon. For more information about individual sights, *see* Chapter 2.

DC with Kids

Head right to the **Washington Monument.** Not only will children enjoy a bird's-eye view of the city, they'll also enjoy watching the ongoing renovation of this historic landmark. From here head to the **National Air and Space Museum**; on the way, you can stop to ride a painted pony at the **carousel** near the Smithsonian castle. If you still have time, visit either the **National Museum of American History** or the **National Museum of Natural History**; both have hands-on rooms for little ones that are open most afternoons.

Georgetown

Explore trendy **Georgetown.** There are sights to see, but people come here mainly to watch other people, shop, eat, and bar-hop.

The Mall

Start at either end of the **Mall**—at the Capitol or the Lincoln Memorial—and walk to the opposite end. You won't have time to see everything along the way, but you'll walk past or have in sight most of the attractions Washington is famous for: the **Lincoln Memorial,** the **Vietnam**

Veterans Memorial, the **Tidal Basin** and **Jefferson Memorial**, the **Washington Monument** (and to the north, the **White House**), most of the **Smithsonian museums**, the **National Gallery of Art**, and the **Capitol**.

The Smithsonian

Spend some time at one or two museums—a few don't-misses are the **National Museum of Natural History**, the **National Air and Space Museum**, and the **United States Holocaust Memorial Museum**.

2 Exploring Washington, DC

By John F.
Kelly

Updated
by Bruce
Walker

TIRED OF ITS NOMADIC EXISTENCE after having set up shop in eight locations, Congress voted in 1785 to establish a permanent "Federal town." Northern lawmakers wanted the capital on the Delaware River, in the North; Southerners wanted it on the Potomac, in the South. A deal was struck when Virginia's Thomas Jefferson agreed to support the proposal that the federal government assume the war debts of the colonies if New York's Alexander Hamilton and other northern legislators would agree to locate the capital on the banks of the Potomac. George Washington himself selected the site of the capital, a diamond-shape, 100-square-mi plot that encompassed the confluence of the Potomac and Anacostia rivers, not far from his estate at Mount Vernon. To give the young city a head start, Washington included the already thriving tobacco ports of Alexandria, Virginia, and Georgetown, Maryland, in the District of Columbia.

Pierre-Charles L'Enfant, a young French engineer who had fought in the Revolution, offered his services in creating a capital "magnificent enough to grace a great nation". L'Enfant wrote that his 1791 plan would "leave room for that aggrandizement and embellishment which the increase in the wealth of the nation will permit it to pursue at any period, however remote." At times it must have seemed remote indeed, for the town grew so slowly that when Charles Dickens visited Washington in 1842, what he saw were "spacious avenues that begin in nothing and lead nowhere; streets a mile long that only want houses, roads, and inhabitants; public buildings that need but a public to be complete and ornaments of great thoroughfares which need only great thoroughfares to ornament."

It took the Civil War—and every war thereafter—to energize the city, by attracting thousands of new residents and spurring building booms that extended the capital in all directions. Streets were paved in the 1870s, and the first streetcars ran in the 1880s. Memorials to famous Americans like Lincoln and Jefferson were built in the first decades of the 20th century, along with the massive Federal Triangle, a monument to thousands of less-famous government workers. Despite the District's growth and the fact that blacks have played an important role in the city's history (black mathematician Benjamin Banneker surveyed the land with Pierre L'Enfant), Washington today remains essentially segregated. Whites—who account for about 30% of the population—reside mostly in northwest Washington. Blacks live largely east of Rock Creek Park and south of the Anacostia River.

Washington is a city of other unfortunate contrasts: Citizens of the capital of the free world couldn't vote in a presidential election until 1964, weren't granted limited home rule until 1974, and are represented in Congress by a single nonvoting delegate (though in 1990 residents elected two "shadow" senators, one of whom is political gadfly Jesse Jackson). Homeless people sleep on steam grates next to multimillion-dollar government buildings, and a flourishing drug trade has earned Washington the dubious distinction of murder capital of the United States. Though it's little consolation to those affected, most crime is restricted to neighborhoods far from the areas visited by tourists.

Still, there's no denying that Washington, the world's first planned capital, is also one of its most beautiful. And though the federal government dominates the city psychologically as much as the Washington Monument dominates it physically, there are places where you can leave politics behind. As you explore Washington, look for evidence of L'Enfant's hand, still present despite growing pains and frequent deviations from his plan. His Washington was to be a city of vistas—pleasant views that would shift and change from block to block, a marriage of geometry and art. It remains this way today. Like its main industry, politics, Washington's design is a constantly changing kaleidoscope that invites contemplation from all angles.

The Mall

The Mall is the heart of nearly every visitor's trip to Washington. With nearly a dozen diverse museums ringing the expanse of green, it's the closest thing the capital has to a

Exploring Washington, D.C. *(Boxes Refer to Detail Maps)*

Georgetown

California St.

S St.

Decatur Pl.
R St.

Sheridan
Circle

R St.

Q St.

Massachusetts Ave.

Florida Ave.

TO ADAMS-
MORGAN/
WOODLEY
PARK

**Dupont Circle
and Foggy Bottom**

S St.

Corcoran St.

Q St.

14th St.

Dupont
Circle

Church St.

Church St

P St.

O St.

Rhode Island Ave

P St.

O St.

Rock Creek

30th St.
29th St.
28th St.
27th St.

N St.

22nd St.
21st St.
20th St.
19th St.

17th St.

N St.

Scott
Circle

16th St.

15th St.

Thomas
Circle

M St.

M St.

M St.

M St.

L St.

Washington
Circle

L St.

New Hampshire Ave.

Connecticut Ave.

18th St.

**The White
House Area**

K St.

25th St.

Pennsylvania

Ave.

H St.

New York

24th St.

23rd St.

22nd St.

G St.

F St.

E St.

Virginia Ave.

17th St.

**The White
House**

15th St.

14th St.

D St.

C St.

Constitution Ave.

**Lincoln
Memorial**

Reflecting Pool

**Washington
Monument**

Arlington Memorial Br.

Independence Ave.

Kutz Br.

Tidal Basin

Columbia
Island

West Potomac Park

W. Basin Dr.

Outlet Br.

Ohio Dr.

Lady Bird Johnson Park

Potomac River

**Jefferson
Memorial**

TO
ALEXANDRIA

The Monuments

NW ◆ NE

S St.

S St.

R St.

Rhode Island Ave.

Vermont Ave.

Florida Ave.

Q St.

R St.

New Jersey Ave.

Lincoln Rd.

Q St.

P St.

Q St.

9th St.

8th St.

7th St.

6th St.

3rd St.

1st St.

O St.

N St.

4th St.

New York Ave.

1st St.

O St.

N St.

10th St.

11th St.

12th St.

M St.

M St.

L St.

chusetts Ave.

Massachusetts Ave.

3rd St.

Mt. Vernon Square

I St.

H St.

Old Downtown and Federal Triangle

Capitol Hill

G St.

F St.

Union Station
Columbus Memorial Fountain

E St.

2nd St.

D St.

Pennsylvania

Ave.

Louisiana Ave.

Stanton Park

NE ◆ SE

Constitution Ave.

E. Capitol St.

Madison Dr.

National Gallery of Art

THE MALL

Smithsonian Institution

Jefferson Dr.

National Air and Space Museum

US Capitol

Independence Ave.

Maryland Ave.

Folger Park

C St.

Canal St.

The Mall

New Jersey Ave.

D St.

E St.

s Case
ial Br.

Southwest Fwy.

G St.

G St.

0   550 yards
0   500 meters

I St.

Virginia Ave.

N

Washington
Canal

SW ◆ SE

theme park (unless you count the federal government itself, which has uncharitably been called "Disneyland on the
Potomac"). As at a theme park, you may have to stand in
an occasional line, but unlike the amusements at Disneyland, almost everything you'll see here is free. You may, however, need free, timed-entry tickets to some of the more
popular traveling exhibitions. These are usually available
at the museum information desk or by phone, for a service
charge, from Ticketmaster (☎ 202/432–7328).

Of course, the Mall is more than just a front yard for all
these museums. Bounded on the north and south by Constitution and Independence avenues, and on the east and west
by 3rd and 14th streets, it's a picnicking park and a jogging
path, an outdoor stage for festivals and fireworks, and
America's town green. Nine of the Smithsonian Institution's 14 museums in the capital lie within these boundaries.

*Numbers in the margin correspond to numbers on the Mall
map; these indicate a suggested path for sightseeing.*

Sights to See

⑫ Arthur M. Sackler Gallery. When Charles Freer endowed
the gallery that bears his name, he insisted on a few conditions: Objects in the collection could not be loaned out,
nor could objects from outside the collections be put on display. Because of the latter restriction it was necessary to build
a second, complementary museum to house the Asian art
collection of Arthur M. Sackler, a wealthy medical re-
searcher and publisher who began collecting Asian art as
a student in the 1940s. Sackler allowed Smithsonian curators to select 1,000 items from his ample collection and
pledged $4 million toward the construction of the mu-
seum. Articles in the permanent collection include Chinese
ritual bronzes, jade ornaments from the 3rd millennium BC,
Persian manuscripts, and Indian paintings in gold, silver,
lapis lazuli, and malachite. ⊠ *1050 Independence Ave.
SW,* ☎ *202/357–2700 or 202/357–1729 TDD.* ☑ *Free.*
☉ *Daily 10–5:30. Metro: Smithsonian.*

❷ Arts and Industries Building. In 1876 Philadelphia hosted
the United States International Exposition in honor of the
nation's Centennial. After the festivities, scores of exhibitors

donated their displays to the federal government. To house the objects that had suddenly come its way, the Smithsonian commissioned this redbrick-and-sandstone structure, the second Smithsonian museum to be constructed. Designed by Adolph Cluss, the building was originally called the United States National Museum, the name that's still engraved in stone above the doorway. Some of the objects on display—which include carriages, tools, printing presses, even a steam locomotive—are from the original Philadelphia Centennial. ⊠ *900 Jefferson Dr. SW,* ☎ *202/357–2700 or 202/357–1729 TDD.* ▨ *Free.* ☉ *Daily 10–5:30. Metro: Smithsonian.*

☝ ❾ **Bureau of Engraving and Printing.** Paper money has been printed here since 1914, when they stopped printing it in the Auditor's Building. Despite the fact that there are no free samples, the guided tour of the bureau—which takes you past presses that turn out some $450 million a day— is one of the city's most popular. In addition to all the paper currency in the United States, stamps, military certificates, and presidential invitations are printed here, too. The tour here lasts 40 minutes; the wait to get in can be twice that long. ⊠ *14th and C Sts. SW,* ☎ *202/874–3019.* ▨ *Free; Apr. 3–Sept. same-day timed-entry passes issued starting at 8 AM at Raoul Wallenberg Pl. SW entrance.* ☉ *Sept.–May weekdays 9–2; June–Aug. weekdays 9–2 and 5–7:30. Metro: Smithsonian.*

❿ **Department of Agriculture.** Although there's little of interest to tourists inside, this complex is too gargantuan to ignore. The home of a major governmental agency responsible for setting and carrying out the nation's agricultural policies, it comprises two buildings. ⊠ *Independence Ave. between 12th and 14th Sts. SW. Metro: Smithsonian.*

⓫ **Freer Gallery of Art.** One of the world's finest collections of masterpieces from Asia, the Smithsonian's Freer Gallery of Art was made possible by an endowment from Detroit industrialist Charles L. Freer, who retired in 1900 and devoted the rest of his life to collecting art. Opened in 1923, four years after its benefactor's death, its collection includes more than 26,000 works of art from the Far and Near

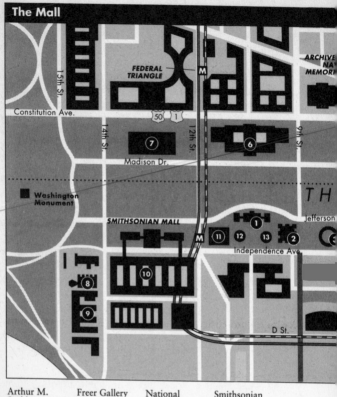

The Mall

15th St.

FEDERAL TRIANGLE

M

ARCHIVE NA' MEMORY

Constitution Ave.

14th St.

12th St.

9th St.

50 1

⑦

Madison Dr.

⑥

■ Washington Monument

T H

SMITHSONIAN MALL

Jefferson

M ⑪ ⑫ ⑬ ① ②

Independence Ave.

⑧

⑩

⑨

D St.

Arthur M. Sackler Gallery, **12**

Arts and Industries Building, **2**

Bureau of Engraving and Printing, **9**

Department of Agriculture, **10**

Freer Gallery of Art, **11**

Hirshhorn Museum and Sculpture Garden, **3**

National Air and Space Museum, **4**

National Gallery of Art, **5**

National Museum of African Art, **13**

National Museum of American History, **7**

National Museum of Natural History, **6**

Smithsonian Institution Building, **1**

United States Holocaust Memorial Museum, **8**

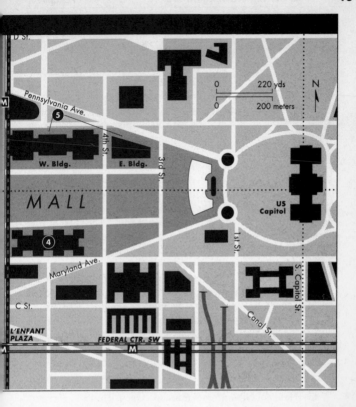

D St.

M

Pennsylvania Ave.

0 ──────── 220 yds

0 ──────── 200 meters

N

⑤

4th St.

3rd St.

W. Bldg.

E. Bldg.

MALL

US Capitol

④

1st St.

S. Capitol St.

Maryland Ave.

C St.

Canal St.

L'ENFANT PLAZA

M

FEDERAL CTR. SW

M

East, including Asian porcelains, Japanese screens, Chinese paintings and bronzes, Korean stoneware, and examples of Islamic art. ✉ *12th St. and Jefferson Dr. SW,* ☎ *202/357–2700 or 202/357–1729 TTD.* 🎫 *Free.* ☉ *Daily 10–5:30. Metro: Smithsonian.*

❸ **Hirshhorn Museum and Sculpture Garden.** An architecturally striking but aesthetically controversial round building that opened in 1974, the Hirshhorn manages a collection that includes 4,000 paintings and drawings and 2,000 sculptures donated by Joseph H. Hirshhorn, a Latvian-born immigrant who made his fortune running uranium mines. Works by such American artists as Thomas Eakins, Jackson Pollock, and Mark Rothko are represented, as are modern European and Latin masters, including Francis Bacon, Fernando Botero, and Joan Miró. The Hirshhorn's impressive sculpture collection is displayed throughout the museum, as well as in the open spaces between the museum's concrete piers and across Jefferson Drive in the sunken **Sculpture Garden.** The display in the garden includes one of the largest public American collections of works by Henry Moore, as well as works by Honoré Daumier, Max Ernst, Alberto Giacometti, Pablo Picasso, and Man Ray. Auguste Rodin's *Burghers of Calais* is a highlight. ✉ *Independence Ave. and 7th St. SW,* ☎ *202/357–2700 or 202/357–1729 TDD.* 🎫 *Free.* ☉ *Museum daily 10–5:30, sculpture garden daily 7:30–dusk. Metro: Smithsonian.*

★ ☪ ❹ **National Air and Space Museum.** Opened in 1976, this museum attracts more than 8 million people each year. Its 23 galleries tell the story of aviation from the earliest human attempts at flight. Suspended from the ceiling like plastic models in a child's room are dozens of aircraft, including the 1903 *Wright Flyer* that Wilbur Wright piloted over the sands of Kitty Hawk, North Carolina; Charles Lindbergh's *Spirit of St. Louis;* the X-1 rocket plane in which Chuck Yeager broke the sound barrier; and an X-15, the first aircraft to exceed Mach 6. Upstairs, the **Albert Einstein Planetarium,** which charges a small fee, projects images of celestial bodies on a domed ceiling. ✉ *Independence Ave. and 6th St. SW,* ☎ *202/357–2700, 202/357–1729 TDD, or 202/357–1686 for movie information.* 🎫 *Free.* ☉ *Daily 10–5:30. Metro: Smithsonian.*

★ ❺ **National Gallery of Art.** The two buildings of the National Gallery hold one of the world's foremost collections of paintings, sculptures, and graphics. If you want to view the museum's holdings in (more or less) chronological order, it's best to start your exploration in the **West Building.** Opened in 1941, the domed West Building was a gift to the nation from financier Andrew Mellon. In 1931, when the Soviet government was short on cash and selling off many of its art treasures, Mellon bought more than $6 million worth of old masters, including Raphael's *The Alba Madonna* and Sandro Botticelli's *Adoration of the Magi.* Mellon promised his collection to America in 1936, the year before his death. He also donated the funds for the construction of the huge gallery and resisted suggestions it be named after him. The West Building's **Rotunda,** with its 24 marble columns surrounding a fountain topped with a statue of Mercury, sets the stage for the masterpieces on display in more than 100 galleries.

The **East Building** opened in 1978 in response to the changing needs of the National Gallery. The atrium is dominated by Alexander Calder's mobile *Untitled,* and the galleries display modern art, though you'll also find major temporary exhibitions that span years and artistic styles. Works include Picasso's *The Lovers* and *Family of Saltimbanques,* four of Henri Matisse's cutouts, Miró's *The Farm,* and Pollock's *Lavender Mist.*

The National Gallery Sculpture Garden opened in the fall of 1998. Granite walkways take you through the garden, which is planted with shade trees, flowering trees, and perennials. Sculptures on display from the museum's permanent collection include Alexander Archipenko's *Woman Combing Her Hair,* Miro's *Personnage Gothique, Oiseau-Eclair,* and Isamu Noguchi's *Great Rock of Inner Seeking.* ⊠ *Constitution Ave. between 3rd and 7th Sts. NW,* ☎ *202/ 737–4215 or 202/842–6176 TDD.* ▣ *Free.* ☉ *Mon.–Sat. 10–5, Sun. 11–6. Metro: Archives/Navy Memorial.*

❸ **National Museum of African Art.** Founded in 1964 as a private educational institution dedicated to the collection, exhibition, and study of the traditional arts of Africa, this museum holds more than 7,000 objects representing hundreds of African cultures. On display are masks, carvings, textiles, and jewelry, all made from materials such as wood, fiber, bronze, ivory, and fired clay. ✉ *950 Independence Ave. SW,* ☎ *202/357–2700 or 202/357–1729 TDD.* ✉ *Free.* ☉ *Daily 10–5:30. Metro: Smithsonian.*

⑦ National Museum of American History. Opened in 1964 as the National Museum of History and Technology and re-named in 1980, the museum explores America's cultural, political, technical, and scientific past. The incredible diversity of artifacts helps the Smithsonian live up to its nickname "the Nation's attic." This is the museum that displayed Muhammad Ali's boxing gloves, Judy Garland's ruby slippers from *The Wizard of Oz,* and the Bunkers' living-room furniture from *All in the Family.* On the first floor, the permanent "Science in American Life" exhibit shows how such scientific breakthroughs as the mass production of penicillin and the development of plastics have shaped American life. The second floor is devoted to U.S. social and political history. A permanent exhibit, "First Ladies: Political Role and Public Image," displays gowns worn by presidential wives, but it goes beyond fashion to explore the women behind the satin, lace, and brocade. The third floor has installations on money, musical instruments, and photography. If you want a more interactive visit, check out the **Hands On History Room,** where you can ride a high-wheeler bike or pluck an old stringed instrument. In the **Hands On Science Room** you can do one of 25 experiments, including testing a water sample and exploring DNA fingerprinting. ✉ *Constitution Ave. and 14th St. NW,* ☎ *202/357–2700 or 202/357–1729 TDD.* ✉ *Free.* ☉ *Daily 10–5:30, Hands On History Room Tues.–Sun. noon–3, Hands On Science Room daily 10–5:30. Metro: Smithsonian.*

★ ⑥ National Museum of Natural History. Constructed in 1910, this is one of the great natural history museums in the world, filled with bones, fossils, stuffed animals, and other natural delights—122 million specimens in all. The first-floor rotunda is dominated by a stuffed, 8-ton, 13-ft African bull elephant, one of the largest ever found. Off to the right is the popular **Dinosaur Hall.** Fossilized skeletons here range from a 90-ft-long diplodocus to a tiny thesalosaurus

neglectus (a small dinosaur so named because its discon-
nected bones sat for years in a college drawer before being
reassembled). In the west wing are displays of birds, mam-
mals, and sea life. If you've always wished you could get
your hands on the objects behind the glass, stop by the **Discovery Room,** in the northwest corner of the first floor. Here
elephant tusks, petrified wood, seashells, rocks, feathers,
and other items can be handled.

The highlight of the second floor is the newly reinstalled
**Janet Annenberg Hooker Hall of Geology, Gems and Min-
erals.** Objects include a pair of Marie Antoinette's ear-
rings, the Rosser Reeves ruby, spectacular crystals and
minerals, and, of course, the Hope Diamond, a blue gem
found in India and reputed to carry a curse (though Smithsonian guides are quick to pooh-pooh this notion). Also on
the second floor is the **O. Orkin Insect Zoo,** featuring a walk
through a rain forest and at least 60 species of live insects,
from bees to tarantulas. ⊠ *Constitution Ave. and 10th St.
NW,* ☎ *202/357-2700 or 202/357-1729 TDD.* ▣ *Free.*
⊙ *Daily 10-5:30; Discovery Room Tues.-Fri. noon-2:30,
weekends 10:30-3:30; in spring and summer free passes
distributed starting at 11:45 weekdays, 10:15 weekends.
Metro: Smithsonian.*

❶ **Smithsonian Institution Building.** The first Smithsonian museum constructed, this red sandstone, Norman-style building is better known as the Castle. It was designed by James
Renwick, the architect of St. Patrick's Cathedral in New
York City. Although British scientist and founder James
Smithson had never visited America, his will stipulated
that, should his nephew, Henry James Hungerford, die
without an heir, Smithson's entire fortune would go to the
United States, "to found at Washington, under the name
of the Smithsonian Institution, an establishment for the increase and diffusion of knowledge among men."

Smithson died in 1829, Hungerford in 1835, and in 1838
the United States received $515,169 worth of gold
sovereigns. After eight years of congressional debate over
the propriety of accepting funds from a citizen of another
country, the Smithsonian Institution was finally established
on August 10, 1846. The Castle building was completed

in 1855 and originally housed all of the Smithsonian's operations, including the science and art collections, research laboratories, and living quarters for the institution's secretary and his family. Today the Castle houses Smithsonian administrative offices and the **Smithsonian Information Center.** A 20-minute video provides an overview of the Smithsonian museums and the National Zoo and monitors display information on the day's events. The center opens at 9 AM, an hour before the other museums, so you can plan your day on the Mall without wasting valuable sight-seeing time. ✉ *1000 Jefferson Dr. SW,* ☎ *202/357–2700 or 202/357–1729 TDD.* 🎫 *Free.* ☉ *Daily 9–5:30. Metro: Smithsonian.*

★ ❾ **United States Holocaust Memorial Museum.** Museums usually celebrate the best that humanity can achieve, but this James Ingo Freed–designed museum instead illustrates the worst. A permanent exhibition tells the stories of the millions of Jews, Gypsies, Jehovah's Witnesses, homosexuals, political prisoners, and others killed by the Nazis between 1933 and 1945. Striving to give a you-are-there experience, the graphic presentation is as extraordinary as the subject matter: Upon arrival, you're issued an "identity card" containing biographical information on a real person from the Holocaust. As you move through the museum, you read sequential updates on their cards. The museum recounts the Holocaust with documentary films, videotaped and audiotaped oral histories, and a collection that includes such items as a freight car like those used to transport Jews from Warsaw to the Treblinka death camp, and the Star of David patches that Jewish prisoners were made to wear. Like the history it covers, the museum can be profoundly disturbing; it's not recommended for visitors under 11. Plan to spend at least four hours here. ✉ *100 Raoul Wallenberg Pl. SW (enter from Raoul Wallenberg Pl. or 14th St. SW),* ☎ *202/488–0400 or 703/218–6500 for Protix.* 🎫 *Free, although same-day timed-entry passes necessary for the permanent exhibition.* ☉ *Daily 10–5:30. Metro: Smithsonian.*

The Monuments

Washington is a city of monuments. In the middle of traffic circles, on tiny slivers of park, and at street corners and intersections, statues, plaques, and simple blocks of marble honor the generals, politicians, poets, and statesmen who helped shape the nation. The monuments dedicated to the most famous Americans are west of the Mall on ground reclaimed from the marshy flats of the Potomac. This is also the location of Washington's cherry trees, gifts from Japan.

Numbers in the margin correspond to numbers on the Monuments map; these indicate a suggested path for sightseeing.

Sights to See

➐ Constitution Gardens. Many ideas were proposed to develop a 50-acre site that was once home to "temporary" buildings erected by the navy before World War I and not removed until after World War II. President Nixon is said to have favored something resembling Copenhagen's Tivoli Gardens. The final design was a little plainer, with paths winding through groves of trees and, on the lake, a tiny island paying tribute to the signers of the Declaration of Independence, their signatures carved into a low stone wall. ✉ *Constitution Ave. between 17th and 23rd Sts. NW.* 🖼 *Free. Metro: Foggy Bottom.*

➍ Franklin Delano Roosevelt Memorial. This is the District's newest monument, unveiled in May 1997. The 7½-acre memorial to the 32nd president features waterfalls and reflection pools, four outdoor gallery rooms—each symbolizing one of his four terms as president—and 10 bronze sculptures. The granite passageways that connect the galleries are engraved with some of Roosevelt's most famous quotes, including, "The only thing we have to fear is fear itself." ✉ *West side of Tidal Basin,* ☎ *202/619–7222.* 🖼 *Free.* ☉ *24 hrs.; staffed daily 8 AM–midnight.*

➌ Jefferson Memorial. Congress decided that Jefferson deserved a monument positioned as prominently as those in honor of Washington and Lincoln, and this spot directly south of the White House seemed ideal. Jefferson had always admired the Pantheon in Rome—the rotundas he designed for the University of Virginia and his own Monticello were inspired by its dome—so the memorial's architect, John Russell Pope, drew from the same source. Dedicated in 1943, it houses a statue of Jefferson, and its walls are lined with

20

Constitution
Gardens, **7**

Franklin
Delano
Roosevelt
Memorial, **4**

Jefferson
Memorial, **3**

Lincoln
Memorial, **5**

Lockkeeper's
House, **8**

Tidal Basin, **2**

Vietnam
Veterans
Memorial, **6**

Washington
Monument, **1**

inscriptions based on his writings. One of the best views of the White House can be seen from its top steps. ⊠ *Tidal Basin, south bank,* ☎ *202/426–6821.* 🎟 *Free.* ☉ *Daily 8 AM–midnight. Metro: Smithsonian.*

★ ❺ **Lincoln Memorial.** The white Colorado-marble memorial was designed by Henry Bacon and completed in 1922. The 36 Doric columns represent the 36 states in the Union at the time of Lincoln's death; the names of the states appear on the frieze above the columns. Above the frieze are the names of the 48 states in the Union when the memorial was dedicated. Daniel Chester French's somber statue of the seated president, in the center of the memorial, gazes out over the Reflecting Pool. Though the 19-ft-high sculpture looks as if it were cut from one huge block of stone, it actually comprises 28 interlocking pieces of Georgia marble. Inscribed on the south wall is the Gettysburg Address, and on the north wall is Lincoln's second inaugural address. The best time to see the memorial is at night: spotlights illuminate the outside, while inside, light and shadows play across Lincoln's gentle face. ⊠ *West end of Mall,* ☎ *202/426–6895.* 🎟 *Free.* ☉ *24 hrs; staffed daily 8 AM–midnight. Metro: Foggy Bottom.*

❽ **Lockkeeper's House.** The stone Lockkeeper's House is the only remaining monument to Washington's unsuccessful experiment with a canal. L'Enfant's design called for a canal to be dug from the Tiber—a branch of the Potomac that extended from where the Lincoln Memorial is now—across the city to the Capitol and then south to the Anacostia River. The stone building at this corner was the home of the canal's lockkeeper until the 1870s, when the waterway was covered over with B Street, which was renamed Constitution Avenue in 1932. ⊠ *Constitution Ave. and 17th St. Metro: Federal Triangle, 5 blocks east on 12th St.*

🔄 ❷ **Tidal Basin.** This placid pond was part of the Potomac until 1882, when portions of the river were filled in to improve navigation and create additional parkland, including that upon which the Jefferson Memorial was later built. You can rent a paddleboat at the boathouse on the east side of the basin, southwest of the Bureau of Engraving. Walking along the sidewalk that hugs the basin, you'll see two grotesque sculpted heads on the sides of the Inlet Bridge. The inside walls of the bridge also sport two other interesting sculptures: bronze, human-headed fish that spout water from their mouths. The bridge was refurbished in the 1980s at the same time the chief of the park—a Mr. Jack Fish—was retiring. Sculptor Constantine Sephralis played a little joke: These fish heads are actually Fish's head. Once you cross the bridge, you can head left, along the Potomac, or continue along the Tidal Basin to the right. The latter route is somewhat more scenic, especially when the cherry trees are in bloom. The first batch of these trees arrived from Japan in 1909. About 200 of the original trees still grow near the Tidal Basin, the centerpiece of Washington's Cherry Blossom Festival each spring. The trees are usually in bloom for about 10–12 days at the beginning of April. ✉ *Boathouse: Northeast bank of Tidal Basin,* ☎ *202/479–2426.* 🎫 *Paddleboat rental $7 per hr, $1.75 each additional 15 mins.* ☉ *Mid-Mar.–Oct., daily 10–6 (until 5 in Mar. and Apr.), weather permitting. Metro: Smithsonian.*

❻ **Vietnam Veterans Memorial.** Renowned for its power to evoke poignant reflection, the Vietnam Veterans Memorial was conceived by Jan Scruggs, a former infantry corporal who had served in Vietnam. The stark design by Maya Ying Lin, a 21-year-old Yale architecture student, was selected in a 1981 competition. The wall is one of the most visited sites in Washington, its black granite panels reflecting the sky, the trees, and the faces of those looking for the names of friends or relatives who died in the war. The names of more than 58,000 Americans are etched on the face of the memorial in the order of their deaths. Directories at the entrance and exit to the wall list the names in alphabetical order. For help in finding a name, ask a ranger at the blue-and-white hut near the entrance. Tents are often set up near the wall by veterans groups; some provide information on soldiers who remain missing in action, and others are on call to help fellow vets deal with the sometimes overwhelming emotions that grip them when visiting the wall for the first time. ✉ *Constitution Gardens, 23rd St. and Constitution Ave. NW,* ☎ *202/634–1568.* 🎫 *Free.* ☉ *24 hrs; staffed daily 8 AM–midnight. Metro: Foggy Bottom.*

Vietnam Women's Memorial. After years of debate over its design and necessity, the Vietnam Women's Memorial, honoring the women who served in that conflict, was finally dedicated on Veterans Day 1993. It is a stirring sculpture group consisting of two uniformed women caring for a wounded male soldier while a third woman kneels nearby. ⊠ *Constitution Gardens, southeast of Vietnam Veterans Memorial.* ▨ *Free. Metro: Foggy Bottom.*

🖐 ❶ **Washington Monument.** Congress first authorized a monument to General Washington in 1783. In his 1791 plan for the city, Pierre L'Enfant selected a site (the point where a line drawn west from the Capitol crossed one drawn south from the White House), but it wasn't until 1833, after years of quibbling in Congress, that a private National Monument Society was formed to select a designer and to search for funds. Robert Mills's winning design called for a 600-ft-tall decorated obelisk rising from a circular colonnaded building. The building at the base was to be an American pantheon, adorned with statues of national heroes and a massive statue of Washington riding in a chariot pulled by snorting horses.

Because of the marshy conditions of L'Enfant's original site, the position of the monument was shifted to firmer ground 100 yards southeast. (If you walk a few steps north of the monument you can see the stone marker that denotes L'Enfant's original axis.) The cornerstone was laid in 1848 with the same Masonic trowel Washington himself had used to lay the Capitol's cornerstone 55 years earlier. The National Monument Society continued to raise funds after construction was begun, soliciting subscriptions of $1 from citizens across America. It also urged states, organizations, and foreign governments to contribute memorial stones for the construction. Problems arose in 1854, when members of the anti-Papist "Know Nothing" party stole a block donated by Pope Pius IX, smashed it, and dumped its shards into the Potomac. This action, a lack of funds, and the onset of the Civil War kept the monument at a fraction of its final height, open at the top, and vulnerable to the rain. A clearly visible ring about a third of the way up the obelisk testifies to this unfortunate stage of the monument's history:

Although all of the marble in the obelisk came from the same Maryland quarry, that used for the second phase of construction came from a different stratum and is of a slightly different shade.

In 1876 Congress finally appropriated $200,000 to finish the monument, and the Army Corps of Engineers took over construction; work was finally completed in December 1884, when the monument was topped with a 7½-pound piece of aluminum, then one of the most expensive metals in the world. Four years later the monument was opened to visitors, who rode to the top in a steam-operated elevator. (Only men were allowed to take the 20-minute ride; it was thought too dangerous for women, who as a result had to walk up the stairs if they wanted to see the view.)

A major renovation project was begun in 1998. The monument was closed for four months while the heating and cooling systems were replaced and the elevator was serviced. Work on the exterior, including a close inspection and cleaning of the surfaces and replacement of the mortar between the 36,000 slabs of marble, will continue until 2000. During that time the monument will be wrapped in transparent blue fabric that masks the scaffolding.

At 555 ft, 5 inches, the Washington Monument is the world's tallest masonry structure. The view from the top takes in most of the District and parts of Maryland and Virginia. You are no longer permitted to climb the 898 steps leading to the top. Most spring and summer weekends there are walk-down tours at 10 and 2, with a guide describing the monument's construction and showing the 193 stone and metal plaques that adorn the inside. (The tours are sometimes canceled due to lack of staff. Call the day of your visit to confirm.) To avoid the formerly long lines of people waiting for the minute-long elevator ride up the monument's shaft, the park service now uses a free timed-ticket system. A limited number of tickets are available at the kiosk on 15th Street daily beginning at 7:30 AM April–Labor Day and 8:30 AM September–March, with a limit of six tickets per person. Tickets are good during a specified half-hour period. No tickets are required after 8 PM (3

PM in the off-season). Advance tickets are available from Ticketmaster (call 202/432–7328; $1.50 per ticket service charge). ⊠ *Constitution Ave. and 15th St. NW*, ☎ *202/426–6840*. ⊠ *Free*. ☉ *Apr.–Labor Day, daily 8 AM–midnight; Sept.–Mar., daily 9–5. Metro: Smithsonian.*

The White House Area

In a world full of recognizable images, few are better known than the whitewashed, 32-room, Irish-country-house–like mansion at 1600 Pennsylvania Avenue. The residence of arguably the single most powerful person on the planet, the White House has an awesome majesty, having been the home of every U.S. president except, ironically, the father of our country, George Washington. This is where the buck stops in America and where the nation turns in times of crisis. After joining the more than 1.5 million people who visit the White House each year, strike out into the surrounding streets to explore the president's neighborhood, which includes some of the city's oldest houses.

Numbers in the margin correspond to numbers on the White House Area map; these indicate a suggested path for sightseeing.

Sights to See

13 **Art Museum of the Americas.** This small gallery has changing exhibits highlighting 20th-century Latin American artists. ⊠ *201 18th St. NW*, ☎ *202/458–6016*. ⊠ *Free*. ☉ *Tues.–Sun. 10–5. Metro: Farragut West.*

Blair House. A green canopy marks the entrance to Blair House, the residence used by heads of state visiting Washington. Harry S. Truman lived here from 1948 to 1952 while the White House was undergoing renovations. ⊠ *1651 Pennsylvania Ave. Metro: McPherson Square.*

8 **Corcoran Gallery of Art.** The Corcoran is one of the few large museums in Washington outside the Smithsonian family. The Beaux Arts–style building was designed by Ernest Flagg and completed in 1897. The gallery's permanent collection numbers more than 14,000 works, including paintings by the first great American portraitists John

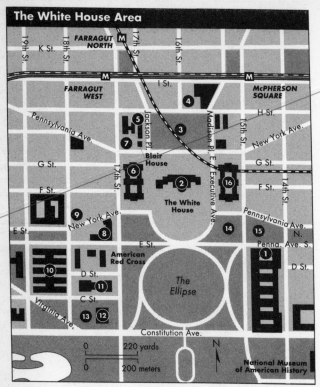

The White House Area

FARRAGUT NORTH

K St.

19th St.
18th St.
17th St.
16th St.

FARRAGUT WEST

I St.

McPHERSON SQUARE

Pennsylvania Ave.

H St.

15th St.

New York Ave.

Jackson Pl.

Madison Pl.

G St.

G St.

Blair House

14th St.

F St.

F St.

17th St.

The White House

E. Executive Ave.

New York Ave.

E St.

Pennsylvania Ave. N.

E St.

Penna. Ave. S.

American Red Cross

The Ellipse

D St.

D St.

C St.

Virginia Ave.

Constitution Ave.

0   220 yards
0   200 meters

N

National Museum of American History

Art Museum of the Americas, **13**

Corcoran Gallery of Art, **8**

DAR Museum, **11**

Decatur House, **5**

Department of the Interior, **10**

Lafayette Square, **3**

Octagon, **9**

Old Executive Office Building, **6**

Organization of American States, **12**

Pershing Park, **15**

Renwick Gallery, **7**

St. John's Episcopal Church, **4**

Treasury Building, **16**

White House, **2**

White House Visitor Center, **1**

William Tecumseh Sherman Monument, **14**

Copley, Gilbert Stuart, and Rembrandt Peale. The Hudson River school is represented by such works as *Mount Corcoran* by Albert Bierstadt and Frederic Church's *Niagara*. There are also portraits by John Singer Sargent, Eakins, and Cassatt. European art is seen in the Walker Collection (late-19th- and early 20th-century paintings, including works by Gustave Courbet, Monet, Camille Pissarro, and Renoir) and the Clark Collection (Dutch, Flemish, and French Romantic paintings, and the restored entire 18th-century Salon Doré of the Hotel d'Orsay in Paris). Photography and works by contemporary American artists are also among the Corcoran's strengths. ⊠ *500 17th St. NW,* ☎ *202/639–1700.* 🖼 *Suggested donation $3.* ☉ *Mon., Wed., and Fri.–Sun. 10–5; Thurs. 10–9; tours of permanent collection Mon.–Wed. and Fri. at noon; Sat.–Sun. at 10:30 AM, noon, and 2:30 PM; Thurs. at 7:30 PM. Metro: Farragut West or Farragut North.*

🐾 ⓫ **DAR Museum.** A Beaux Arts building serving as headquarters of the Daughters of the American Revolution, Memorial Continental Hall was the site of the DAR's annual congress until the larger Constitution Hall was built around the corner. An entrance on D Street leads to the DAR Museum. Its 33,000-item collection includes fine examples of Colonial and Federal furniture, textiles, quilts, silver, china, porcelain, stoneware, earthenware, and glass. Thirty-three period rooms are decorated in styles representative of various U.S. states. ⊠ *1776 D St. NW,* ☎ *202/879–3240.* 🖼 *Free.* ☉ *Weekdays 8:30–4, Sun. 1–5. Metro: Farragut West.*

❺ **Decatur House.** Designed by Benjamin Latrobe, Decatur House was built for naval hero Stephen Decatur and his wife, Susan, in 1819. A redbrick, Federal-style building on the corner of H Street and Jackson Place, it was the first private residence on President's Park. Later occupants of the house included Henry Clay, Martin Van Buren, and the Beales, a prominent family from the West whose modifications of the building include a parquet floor showing the state seal of California. The house is now operated by the National Trust for Historic Preservation. The first floor is furnished as it was in Decatur's time. The second floor is furnished in the Victorian style favored by the Beale family, who owned

it until 1956. ⊠ *748 Jackson Pl. NW,* ☎ *202/842–0920.*
▱ *$4.* ☉ *Tues.–Fri. 10–3, weekends noon–4; tours on the hr and ½ hr. Metro: Farragut West.*

🔟 **Department of the Interior.** Designed by Waddy B. Wood, the Department of the Interior was the most modern government building in the city and the first with escalators and central air-conditioning at the time of its construction in 1937. The outside of the building is somewhat plain, but much of the inside is decorated with murals that reflect the department's work. You'll pass several of these if you visit the **Department of the Interior Museum** on the first floor. (You can enter the building at its E Street or C Street door; adults must show photo ID.) Exhibits outline the work of the Bureau of Land Management, the U.S. Geological Survey, the Bureau of Indian Affairs, the National Park Service, and other department branches. ⊠ *C and E Sts. between 18th and 19th Sts. NW,* ☎ *202/208–4743.* ▱ *Free.* ☉ *Weekdays 8–5. Metro: Farragut West.*

③ **Lafayette Square.** Pierre L'Enfant's original plan for the city designated this area as part of "President's Park"; in essence it was the president's front yard, just as what is now the Ellipse was once the president's backyard. The egalitarian Thomas Jefferson, concerned that large, landscaped White House grounds would give the wrong impression in a democratic country, ordered that the area be turned into a public park. In the center of the park—and dominating the square—is a large **statue of Andrew Jackson.** Erected in 1853 and cast from bronze cannons that Jackson captured during the War of 1812, this was the first equestrian statue made in America. Jackson's is the only statue of an American in the park. In the southeast corner is the park's namesake, the **Marquis de Lafayette,** the young French nobleman who came to America to fight in the Revolution. The modern redbrick building at 717 Madison Place houses judicial offices. Its design—with squared-off bay windows—is echoed in the taller building that rises behind it and is mirrored in the **New Executive Office Building** on the other side of Lafayette Square. The yellow house next door, with a second-story ironwork balcony, was built in 1828 by Benjamin Ogle Tayloe. During the McKinley administration, Ohio senator Marcus Hanna lived here, and the president's frequent visits earned it the nickname the "Little White House." ⊠ *Bounded by Pennsylvania Ave., Madison Pl., H St., and Jackson Pl. Metro: McPherson Square.*

⑨ Octagon. This octagon actually has six, rather than eight, sides. Designed by Dr. William Thornton (the Capitol's architect), it was built for John Tayloe III, a wealthy Virginia plantation owner, and was completed in 1801. After the White House was burned in 1814 the Tayloes invited James and Dolley Madison to stay in the Octagon. It was in a second-floor study that the Treaty of Ghent, ending the War of 1812, was signed. It is now the **museum of the American Architectural Foundation.** The galleries inside host changing exhibits on architecture, city planning, and Washington history and design. ⊠ *1799 New York Ave. NW,* ☎ *202/638–3105 or 202/638–1538 TDD.* ▣ *$3.* ☉ *Tues.–Sun. 10–4. Metro: Farragut West.*

⑥ Old Executive Office Building. Once one of the most detested buildings in the city, the Old Executive Office Building is now one of the most beloved. It was built between 1871 and 1888 and originally housed the War, Navy, and State departments. Its architect, Alfred B. Mullett, patterned it after the Louvre, but detractors quickly criticized the busy French Empire design—with its mansard roof, tall chimneys, and 900 freestanding columns—as an inappropriate counterpoint to the Greek Revival Treasury Building that sits on the other side of the White House. The Old Executive Office Building has hosted numerous historic events. It was here that Secretary of State Cordell Hull met with Japanese diplomats after the bombing of Pearl Harbor, and it was here that Oliver North and Fawn Hall shredded Iran-Contra documents. ⊠ *Across Pennsylvania Ave. west of White House. Metro: Farragut West.*

⑫ Organization of American States. The headquarters of the Organization of American States, which is made up of nations from North, South, and Central America, contains a cool patio adorned with a pre-Columbian–style fountain and lush tropical plants. ⊠ *17th St. and Constitution Ave. NW,* ☎ *202/458–3000.* ▣ *Free.* ☉ *Weekdays 9–5:30. Metro: Farragut West.*

⑮ **Pershing Park.** A quiet sunken garden honors General "Blackjack" Pershing, famed for his failed attempt to capture the Mexican revolutionary Pancho Villa in 1916–17 and then for commanding the American expeditionary force in World War I, among other military exploits. Engravings on the stone walls recount pivotal campaigns from that war. ⊠ *15th St. and Pennsylvania Ave. Metro: McPherson Square.*

❼ **Renwick Gallery.** The words "Dedicated to Art" are engraved above the entrance to the French Second Empire–style building, designed by James Renwick in 1859 to house the art collection of Washington merchant and banker William Wilson Corcoran. Corcoran was a Southern sympathizer who spent the duration of the Civil War in Europe. While he was away, his unfinished building was pressed into service by the government as a quartermaster general's post. In 1874 the Corcoran, as it was then called, opened as the first private art museum in the city. Corcoran's collection quickly outgrew the building, and in 1897 it was moved to a new gallery a few blocks south on 17th Street (☞ Corcoran Gallery of Art, *above*). After a stint as the U.S. Court of Claims, this building was restored, renamed after its architect, and opened in 1972 as the Smithsonian's Museum of American Crafts. Not everything in the museum is Shaker furniture and enamel jewelry, though. The second-floor Grand Salon is still furnished in the opulent Victorian style Corcoran favored when his collection adorned its walls. ⊠ *Pennsylvania Ave. and 17th St. NW,* ☎ *202/357–2700 or 202/357–1729 TDD.* ▧ *Free.* ☉ *Daily 10–5:30. Metro: Farragut West.*

❹ **St. John's Episcopal Church.** The golden-domed so-called Church of the Presidents sits across Lafayette Park from the White House. Every president since Madison has visited the church, and many worshiped here regularly. Built in 1816, the church was the second building on the square. Benjamin Latrobe, who worked on both the Capitol and the White House, designed it in the form of a Greek cross, with a flat dome and a lantern cupola. Not far from the center of the church is Pew 54, where visiting presidents are seated. ⊠ *16th and H Sts. NW,* ☎ *202/347–8766.* ▧

Free. ☉ *Weekdays 9–3; guided tours by appointment. Metro: McPherson Square.*

16 **Treasury Building.** Construction of the Treasury Building started in 1836 and, after several additions, was finally completed in 1869. Its southern facade has a **statue of Alexander Hamilton**, the department's first secretary. Guided 90-minute tours—given every Saturday, except holiday weekends, at 10, 10:20, 10:40, and 11—take you past the Andrew Johnson Suite, used by Johnson as the executive office while Mrs. Lincoln moved out of the White House; the two-story marble Cash Room; and a 19th-century burglarproof vault lining that saw duty when the building stored currency. Register at least one week ahead for the tour; you must provide name, date of birth, and Social Security number and show a photo ID at the start of the tour. ✉ *15th St. and Pennsylvania Ave. NW,* ☎ *202/622–0896 or 202/622–0692 TDD.* 🎫 *Free. Metro: McPherson Square.*

★ ☙ **2** **White House.** Pierre L'Enfant called it the President's House; it was known formally as the Executive Mansion; and in 1902 Congress officially proclaimed it the White House, though, contrary to popular belief, it had been given that nickname even before its white sandstone exterior was painted to cover the fire damage it suffered during the War of 1812. Irishman James Hoban's plan, based on the Georgian design of Leinster Hall in Dublin and of other Irish country houses, was selected in a 1792 contest. The building wasn't ready for its first occupant, John Adams, the second U.S. president, until 1800, and so, in a colossal irony, George Washington, who seems to have slept everyplace else, never slept here. Completed in 1829, it has undergone many structural changes since then: Thomas Jefferson, who had entered his own design in the contest under an assumed name, added terraces to the east and west wings. Andrew Jackson installed running water. James Garfield put in the first elevator. Between 1948 and 1952, Harry Truman had the entire structure gutted and restored, adding a second-story porch to the south portico. George Bush installed a horseshoe pit. Most recently, Bill Clinton had a customized jogging track put in.

Tuesday through Saturday mornings (except holidays), from 10 AM to noon, selected public rooms on the ground floor and first floor are open to visitors. There are two ways to visit the White House. The most popular (and easiest) way is to pick up timed tickets from the ☞ **White House Visitor Center.** Plan on being there 5–10 minutes before your tour is scheduled to begin. The other option is to write to your representative or senator's office 8–10 weeks in advance of your trip to request special VIP passes for tours between 8 and 10 AM, but these tickets are extremely limited. On selected weekends in April and October, the White House is open for garden tours. In December it's decorated for the holidays.

You'll enter the White House through the East Wing lobby on the ground floor, walking past the Jacqueline Kennedy Rose Garden. Your first stop is the large white-and-gold **East Room,** the site of presidential news conferences. In 1814 Dolley Madison saved the room's full-length portrait of George Washington from torch-carrying British soldiers by cutting it from its frame, rolling it up, and spiriting it out of the White House. (No fool she, Dolley also rescued her own portrait.) A later occupant, Teddy Roosevelt, allowed his children to ride their pet pony in the East Room.

The Federal-style **Green Room,** named for the moss-green watered silk that covers its walls, is used for informal receptions and "photo opportunities" with foreign heads of state. Notable furnishings here include a New England sofa that once belonged to Daniel Webster and portraits of Benjamin Franklin, John Quincy Adams, and Abigail Adams. The president and his guests are often shown on TV sitting in front of the Green Room's English Empire mantel, engaging in what are invariably described as "frank and cordial" discussions.

The elliptical **Blue Room,** the most formal space in the White House, is furnished with a gilded Empire-style settee and chairs that were ordered by James Monroe. (Monroe asked for plain wooden chairs, but the furniture manufacturer thought such unadorned furnishings too simple for the White House and took it upon himself to supply chairs more in keeping with their surroundings.)

(Another well-known elliptical room, the president's **Oval Office**, is in the semidetached West Wing of the White House, along with other executive offices.) The **Red Room** is decorated as an American Empire–style parlor of the early 19th century, with furniture by the New York cabinetmaker Charles-Honoré Lannuier. The **State Dining Room**, second in size only to the East Room, can seat 140 guests. It's dominated by G. P. A. Healy's portrait of Abraham Lincoln, painted after the president's death. The stone mantel is inscribed with a quote from one of John Adams's letters: "I pray heaven to bestow the best of blessings on this house and all that shall hereafter inhabit it. May none but honest and wise men ever rule under this roof." ⊠ *1600 Pennsylvania Ave. NW,* ☎ *202/456–7041 or 202/619–7222.* 🎟 *Free.* 🕐 *Tues.–Sat. 10–noon. Metro: Federal Triangle.*

❶ White House Visitor Center. If you're visiting the ☞ **White House,** you need to stop by the visitor center for free tickets. Tickets are dispensed on a first-come, first-served basis. (They're often gone by 9 AM.) Your ticket will show the starting point and approximate time of your tour. Also at the center are exhibits pertaining to the White House's construction, its decor, and the families who have lived there. *Official address:* ⊠ *1450 Pennsylvania Ave. NW; entrance:* ⊠ *Department of Commerce's Baldrige Hall, E St. between 14th and 15th Sts.,* ☎ *202/208–1631.* 🎟 *Free.* 🕐 *Daily 7:30–4. Metro: Federal Triangle.*

⓮ William Tecumseh Sherman Monument. Sherman, whose Atlanta Campaign in 1864 cut a bloody swath of destruction through the Confederacy, was said to be the greatest Civil War general, as the sheer size of this massive monument, set in a small park, would seem to attest. ⊠ *Bounded by E and 15th Sts., East Executive Ave., and Alexander Hamilton Pl. Metro: Federal Triangle.*

Capitol Hill

The people who live and work on "the Hill" do so in the shadow of the edifice that lends the neighborhood its name: the gleaming white Capitol. More than just the center of government, however, the Hill includes charming residential blocks lined with Victorian row houses and a fine assortment of restaurants, bars, and shops. Capitol Hill's boundaries are disputed: It's bordered to the west, north, and south by the Capitol, Union Station, and I Street, respectively. Some argue that Capitol Hill extends east to the Anacostia River, others that it ends at 11th Street near Lincoln Park. The neighborhood does seem to grow as members of Capitol Hill's active historic-preservation movement restore more 19th-century houses. The Capitol also serves as the point from which the city is divided into quadrants: northwest, southwest, northeast, and southeast.

Numbers in the margin correspond to numbers on the Capitol Hill map; these indicate a suggested path for sightseeing.

Sights to See

8 **Bartholdi Fountain.** Frédéric-Auguste Bartholdi, sculptor of the more famous—and much larger—Statue of Liberty, created this delightful fountain, some 25 ft tall, for the Philadelphia Centennial Exhibition of 1876. ⊠ *1st St. and Independence Ave. SW. Metro: Federal Center.*

★ ☙ **3** **Capitol.** As beautiful as the building itself are the Capitol grounds, landscaped in the late 19th century by Frederick Law Olmsted, Sr., who, along with Calvert Vaux, created New York City's Central Park. On these 68 acres you will find both the city's tamest squirrels and the highest concentration of TV news correspondents, vying for a good position in front of the Capitol for their "stand-ups."

The design of this monument was the result of a competition held in 1792; the winner was William Thornton, a physician and amateur architect from the West Indies. The cornerstone was laid by George Washington in a Masonic ceremony on September 18, 1793, and in November 1800, both the Senate and the House of Representatives moved down from Philadelphia to occupy the first completed section: the boxlike portion between the central rotunda and today's north wing. By 1806 the House wing had been completed, just to the south of what is now the domed center, and a covered wooden walkway joined the two wings.

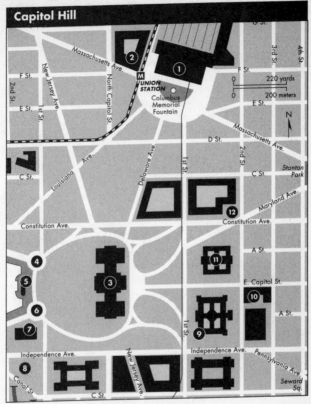

Capitol Hill

Bartholdi
Fountain, **8**

Capitol, **3**

Folger
Shakespeare
Library, **10**

Grant
Memorial, **5**

James Garfield
Memorial, **6**

Library of
Congress, **9**

National Postal
Museum, **2**

Peace
Monument, **4**

Sewall-Belmont
House, **12**

Supreme Court
Building, **11**

Union Station, **1**

United States
Botanic
Garden, **7**

The Congress House grew slowly and suffered a grave setback on August 24, 1814, when British troops led by Sir George Cockburn marched on Washington and set fire to the Capitol, the White House, and numerous other government buildings. The wooden walkway was destroyed and the two wings gutted, but the walls were left standing after a violent rainstorm doused the flames. Architect Benjamin Henry Latrobe supervised the rebuilding of the Capitol, adding such American touches as the corn-cob-and-tobacco-leaf capitals to columns in the east entrance of the Senate wing. He was followed by Boston-born Charles Bulfinch, and in 1826 the Capitol, its low wooden dome sheathed in copper, was finished.

North and south wings were added in the 1850s and '60s to accommodate a growing government trying to keep pace with a growing country. The elongated edifice extended farther north and south than Thornton had planned, and in 1855, to keep the scale correct, work began on a tall cast-iron dome. President Lincoln was criticized for continuing this expensive project while the country was in the throes of the Civil War, but he called the construction "a sign we intend the Union shall go on." The figure atop the dome, often mistaken for Pocahontas, is called *Freedom*.

Guided tours of the Capitol usually start beneath the Rotunda's dome, but if there's a crowd you may have to wait in a line that forms at the top of the center steps on the east side. If you want to forgo the tour, which is brief but informative, you may look around on your own. Enter through one of the lower doors to the right or left of the main steps. Start your exploration under Constantino Brumidi's *Apotheosis of Washington,* in the center of the dome, completed in 1865. The figures in the inner circle represent the 13 original states; those in the outer ring symbolize arts, sciences, and industry. The flat, sculpture-style frieze around the Rotunda's rim was started by Brumidi in 1877. While painting Penn's treaty with the Indians, the 74-year-old artist slipped on the 58-ft-high scaffold and almost fell off. Brumidi managed to hang on until help arrived, but he died a few months later from shock related to the incident. The work was continued by another Italian, Filippo Costaggini, but the frieze wasn't finished until American Allyn Cox added the final touches in 1953.

South of the Rotunda is Statuary Hall, once the legislative chamber of the House of Representatives. The room has an interesting architectural feature that maddened early legislators: A slight whisper uttered on one side of the hall can be heard on the other. (Don't be disappointed if this parlor trick doesn't work when you're visiting the Capitol; sometimes the hall is just too noisy.) To the north, on the Senate side, you can look into the chamber once used by the Supreme Court and into the splendid Old Senate Chamber above it, both of which have been restored. Also be sure to see the Brumidi Corridor on the ground floor of the Senate wing. Frescoes and oil paintings of birds, plants, and American inventions adorn the walls and ceilings, and an intricate, Brumidi-designed bronze stairway leads to the second floor. The Italian artist also memorialized several American heroes, painting them inside trompe l'oeil frames. Trusting that America would continue to produce heroes long after he was gone, Brumidi left some frames empty. The most recent one to be filled, in 1987, honors the crew of the space shuttle *Challenger*.

If you want to watch some of the legislative action in the **House or Senate chambers** while you're on the Hill, you'll have to get a gallery pass from the office of your representative or senator. To find out where those offices are, ask any Capitol police officer, or call ☎ 202/224–3121. In the chambers you'll notice that Democrats sit to the right of the presiding officer, Republicans to the left—the opposite, it's often noted, of their political leanings. The *Washington Post*'s daily "Today in Congress" lists when and where legislative committees are meeting.

When you're finished exploring the inside of the Capitol, make your way to the **west side.** In 1981, Ronald Reagan broke with tradition and moved the presidential swearing-in ceremony to this side of the Capitol, which offers a dramatic view of the Mall and monuments below and can accommodate more guests than the east side, where all previous presidents took the oath of office. ⊠ *East end of Mall,* ☎ *202/224–3121 or 202/225–6827 guide service.* 🎫 *Free.*

🕑 *Daily 9–4:30; summer hrs determined annually, but Rotunda and Statuary Hall usually open daily 9:30–8. Metro: Capitol South or Union Station.*

🔟 Folger Shakespeare Library. The Folger Library's collection of works by and about Shakespeare and his times is second to none. The white-marble Art Deco building, designed by architect Paul Philippe Cret, is decorated with scenes from the Bard's plays. Inside is a reproduction of an inn-yard theater and a gallery, designed in the manner of an Elizabethan Great Hall. ✉ *201 E. Capitol St. SE,* ☎ *202/544–4600.* 🎟 *Free.* 🕑 *Mon.–Sat. 10–4. Metro: Capitol South.*

5️⃣ Grant Memorial. The 252-ft-long memorial to the 16th American president and commander in chief of the Union forces during the Civil War is the largest sculpture group in the city. The statue of Ulysses S. Grant on horseback is flanked by Union artillery and cavalry. ✉ *Near 1st St. and Maryland Ave. SW. Metro: Federal Center.*

6️⃣ James Garfield Memorial. Near the Grant Memorial and the United States Botanic Gardens is a memorial to the 20th president of the United States. James Garfield was assassinated in 1881 after only a few months in office. His bronze statue stands on a pedestal with three other bronze figures seated around it; one bears a tablet inscribed with the words "Law," "Justice," and "Prosperity," which the figures presumably represent. ✉ *1st St. and Maryland Ave. SW. Metro: Federal Center.*

9️⃣ Library of Congress. Provisions for a library to serve members of Congress were originally made in 1800, when the government set aside $5,000 to purchase and house books that legislators might need to consult. This small collection was housed in the Capitol but was destroyed in 1814, when the British burned the city. Thomas Jefferson, then in retirement at Monticello, offered his personal library as a replacement, noting that "there is, in fact, no subject to which a Member of Congress may not have occasion to refer." Jefferson's collection of 6,487 books, for which Congress eventually paid him $23,950, laid the foundation for the great national library.

By the late 1800s it was clear the Capitol could no longer contain the growing library, and the copper-domed **Thomas**

Jefferson Building was constructed. Like many other structures in Washington that seem a bit overwrought (the Old Executive Office Building is another example), the library was criticized when it was completed, in 1897. Busts of Dante, Johann Wolfgang von Goethe, Nathaniel Hawthorne, and other great writers are perched above its entryway. *The Court of Neptune,* Roland Hinton Perry's fountain at the base of the front steps, rivals some of Rome's best fountains. The **Adams Building,** on 2nd Street behind the Jefferson, was added in 1939. A third structure, the **James Madison Building,** opened in 1980; it's just south of the Jefferson Building, between Independence Avenue and C Street.

In 1997, the Jefferson Building, which had been closed for renovations, was reopened to the public. Its Great Hall is richly adorned with mosaics, paintings, and curving marble stairways. But books are only part of the story. Family trees are explored in the Local History and Genealogy Reading Room. In the Folklife Reading Room, researchers can listen to LP recordings of American Indian music or hear the story of B'rer Rabbit read in the Gullah dialect of coastal Georgia and South Carolina. Items from the library's collection—which includes a Gutenberg Bible— are on display in the Jefferson Building's second-floor Southwest Gallery and Pavilion. ⊠ *Jefferson Bldg., 1st St. and Independence Ave. SE,* ☏ *202/707–4604 taped exhibit information, 202/707–5000 Library of Congress operator, or 202/707–6400 taped schedule of general and reading-room hrs.* ▦ *Free.* ☉ *Mon.–Sat. 10–5:30. Tours Mon.– Sat. at 11:30, 1, 2:30, and 4 from Great Hall. Metro: Capitol South.*

🐚 ❷ **National Postal Museum.** Exhibits at this Smithsonian Institute museum underscore the important part the mail has played in the development of America and include horse-drawn mail coaches, railway mail cars, airmail planes, and a collection of philatelic rarities. The museum takes up only a portion of what is the old Washington **City Post Office,** designed by Daniel Burnham and completed in 1914. Nostalgic odes to the noble mail carrier are inscribed on the exterior of the marble building; one of them eulogizes the "Messenger of sympathy and love, servant of parted friends, consoler of the lonely, bond of the scattered family, enlarger of the common life." ⊠ *2 Massachusetts Ave. NE, ☏ 202/ 357–2700 or 202/357–1729 TDD. ▨ Free. ☉ Daily 10– 5:30. Metro: Union Station.*

❹ Peace Monument. A white-marble memorial depicts America in the form of a woman grief-stricken over sailors lost at sea during the Civil War; she is weeping on the shoulder of a second female figure representing History. The plaque inscription refers movingly to navy personnel who "fell in defence of the union and liberty of their country 1861–1865." ⊠ *Traffic circle at 1st St. and Pennsylvania Ave. Metro: Union Station.*

⓬ Sewall-Belmont House. The oldest home on Capitol Hill is now the headquarters of the National Woman's Party. It has a museum that chronicles the early days of the women's movement and is filled with period furniture and portraits and busts of such suffrage-movement leaders as Lucretia Mott, Elizabeth Cady Stanton, and Alice Paul. The redbrick house was built in 1800 by Robert Sewall. Part of the structure dates from the early 1700s. ⊠ *144 Constitution Ave. NE, ☏ 202/546–3989. ▨ Free. ☉ Tues.–Fri. 10–3, Sat. noon–4. Metro: Union Station.*

⓫ Supreme Court Building. It wasn't until 1935 that the Supreme Court got its own building: a white-marble temple with twin rows of Corinthian columns designed by Cass Gilbert. In 1800, the justices arrived in Washington along with the rest of the government but were for years shunted around various rooms in the Capitol; for a while they even met in a tavern. William Howard Taft, the only man to serve as both president and chief justice, was instrumental in getting the court a home of its own, though he died before it was completed.

The Supreme Court convenes on the first Monday in October and remains in session until it has heard all of its cases and handed down all of its decisions (usually the end of June). On Monday through Wednesday of two weeks in each month, the justices hear oral arguments in the velvet-swathed court chamber. Visitors who want to listen can choose to wait in either of two lines. One, the "three-to-five-minute" line, shuttles visitors through, giving them a quick impression of the court at work. If you choose the other, for those who'd like to stay for the whole show, it's best to be in line by 8:30 AM. Perhaps the most interesting appurtenance in the imposing building, however, is a basketball court on one of the upper floors (it's been called the highest court in the land). ⊠ *1st and E. Capitol Sts. NE,* ☎ *202/479–3000.* 🎟 *Free.* ☉ *Weekdays 9–4:30. Metro: Capitol South.*

❶ Union Station. In 1902 the McMillan Commission—charged with suggesting ways to improve the appearance of the city—recommended that the many train lines that sliced through the capital share one main depot. Union Station was opened in 1908 and was the first building completed under the commission's plan. Chicago architect and commission member Daniel H. Burnham patterned the station after the Roman Baths of Diocletian.

The Union Station you see today is the result of a restoration completed in 1988, an effort intended to begin a revival of Washington's east end. It's hoped that the shops, restaurants, and nine-screen movie theater in Union Station will draw more than just train travelers to the Beaux Arts building. The jewel of the structure is its main waiting room. Forty-six statues of Roman legionnaires, one for each state in the Union when the station was completed, ring the grand room. The east hall, now filled with vendors, was once an expensive restaurant. The **Columbus Memorial Fountain,** designed by Lorado Taft, sits in the plaza in front of Union Station. A caped, steely-eyed Christopher Columbus stares into the distance, flanked by a hoary, bearded figure (the Old World) and an Indian brave (the New). ⊠ *Massachusetts Ave. north of Capitol,* ☎ *202/289–1908. Metro: Union Station.*

☞ ❼ United States Botanic Garden. The rather cold exterior belies the peaceful, plant-filled oasis within. The conservatory includes a cactus house, a fern house, and a subtropical house filled with orchids. The conservatory closed in late 1997 for renovation of the building and exhibits. In early 1998, work was begun on the new **National Garden,** which will occupy the 3 acres of lawn adjacent to the conservatory. The conservatory and the garden are scheduled to open in the year 2000. ⊠ *1st St. and Maryland Ave. SW,* ☎ *202/225–8333.* 🎫 *Free.* ☉ *Daily 9–5. Metro: Federal Center SW.*

Old Downtown and Federal Triangle

Nowhere have the city's imperfections been more visible than on L'Enfant's grand thoroughfare, Pennsylvania Avenue. By the early '60s it had become a national disgrace, the dilapidated buildings that lined it home to pawn shops and cheap souvenir stores. While riding up Pennsylvania Avenue in his inaugural parade, a disgusted John F. Kennedy is said to have turned to an aide and said, "Fix it!" Washington's downtown—once within the diamond formed by Massachusetts, Louisiana, Pennsylvania, and New York avenues—had its problems, too, many as a result of the riots that rocked the capital in 1968 after the assassination of Martin Luther King, Jr. In their wake, many businesses left the area and moved north of the White House. In recent years developers have rediscovered "old downtown," and buildings are now being torn down or remodeled at an amazing pace. After several false starts Pennsylvania Avenue is shining once again.

Numbers in the margin correspond to numbers on the Old Downtown and Federal Triangle map; these indicate a suggested path for sightseeing.

Sights to See

❺ Ford's Theatre. In 1861, Baltimore theater impresario John T. Ford leased the First Baptist Church building that stood on this site and turned it into a successful music hall. The building burned down late in 1862, and Ford rebuilt it. The events of April 14, 1865, would shock the nation and close the theater. On that night, during a production of *Our American Cousin,* John Wilkes Booth entered the presidential box and assassinated Abraham Lincoln. The stricken president was carried across the street to the house of tailor William Petersen. Charles Augustus Leale, a 23-year-old doctor, attended to the president, whose injuries would have left him blind had he ever regained consciousness. To let Lincoln know that someone was nearby, Leale held his hand through the night. Lincoln died the next morning.

The federal government bought Ford's Theatre in 1866 for $100,000 and converted it into office space. It was remodeled as a Lincoln museum in 1932 and was restored to its 1865 appearance in 1968. The basement museum—with artifacts such as Booth's pistol and the clothes Lincoln was wearing when he was shot—reopened in 1990. The theater itself continues to present a complete schedule of plays. ⊠ *511 10th St. NW,* ☎ *202/426–6924.* 🎫 *Free.* ☉ *Daily 9–5; theater closed when rehearsals or matinees are in progress (generally Thurs. and weekends); Lincoln Museum in basement remains open at these times. Metro: Metro Center.*

6 **Freedom Plaza.** In 1988, Western Plaza was renamed Freedom Plaza in honor of Dr. Martin Luther King. Its east end is dominated by a **statue of General Casimir Pulaski,** the Polish nobleman who led an American cavalry corps during the Revolutionary War and was mortally wounded in 1779 at the Siege of Savannah. He gazes over a plaza that's inlaid in bronze, a detail from L'Enfant's original 1791 plan for the Federal City. Bronze also outlines the President's Palace and the Congress House; the Mall is represented by a green lawn. To compare L'Enfant's vision with today's reality, stand in the middle of the map's Pennsylvania Avenue and look west. L'Enfant had planned an unbroken vista from the Capitol to the White House, but the Treasury Building, begun in 1836, ruined the view. ⊠ *Bounded by 13th, 14th, and E Sts. and Pennsylvania Ave. Metro: Federal Triangle.*

7 **Friendship Arch.** A colorful and ornate 75-ft-wide arch is a reminder of Washington's sister-city relationship with Beijing. ⊠ *Spanning H St. at 7th Street. Metro: Gallery Place/Chinatown.*

8 **J. Edgar Hoover Federal Bureau of Investigation Building.** The one-hour tour of the FBI building is one of the most popular activities in the city. A brief film outlines the bureau's work, and exhibits describe famous past cases and illustrate the FBI's fight against organized crime, terrorism, bank robbery, es-

Old Downtown and Federal Triangle

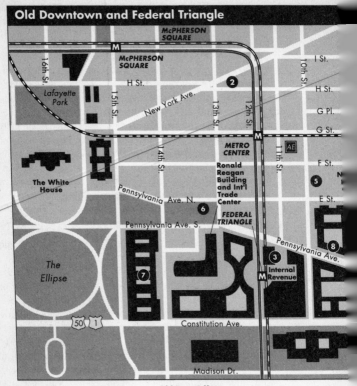

Ford's
Theatre, **5**

Freedom
Plaza, **6**

Friendship
Arch, **1**

J. Edgar
Hoover Federal
Bureau of
Investigation
Building, **8**

National
Aquarium, **7**

National
Archives, **9**

National
Museum of
Women in the
Arts, **2**

Old Patent
Office
Building, **4**

Old Post Office
Building, **3**

KEY

AE American Express Office

pionage, extortion, and other criminal activities. There's everything from gangster John Dillinger's death mask to a poster display of the 10 Most Wanted criminals. You'll also see the laboratories where the FBI painstakingly studies evidence. The high point of the tour comes at the end: An agent gives a live-ammo firearms demonstration in the indoor shooting range. ⊠ *10th St. and Pennsylvania Ave. NW (tour entrance on E St. NW),* ☎ *202/324–3447.* 🎟 *Free.* ☉ *Tours weekdays every 20 min, 8:45–4:15 (note line for tours can be closed on short notice when it gets crowded). Metro: Federal Triangle or Gallery Place/Chinatown.*

☜ ❼ **National Aquarium.** The western base of Federal Triangle between 14th and 15th streets is the home of the Department of Commerce, charged with promoting U.S. economic development and technological advancement. When it opened in 1932 it was the world's largest government office building. It's a good thing there's plenty of space; incongruously, the National Aquarium is housed inside. Established in 1873, it's the country's oldest public aquarium, with more than 1,200 fish and other creatures representing 270 species of fresh- and saltwater life. Its 80 tanks are alive with brilliantly colored tropical fish, firehose-thick moray eels, curious frogs and turtles, silvery schools of flesh-chomping piranhas, and even more fearsome sharks. ⊠ *14th St. and Pennsylvania Ave. NW,* ☎ *202/482–2825.* 🎟 *$2.* ☉ *Daily 9–5; sharks fed Mon., Wed., and Sat. at 2; piranhas fed Tues., Thurs., and Sun. at 2. Metro: Federal Triangle.*

❾ **National Archives.** If the Smithsonian Institution is the nation's attic, the Archives is the nation's basement, and it bears responsibility for the cataloguing and safekeeping of important government documents and other items. The Declaration of Independence, the Constitution, and the Bill of Rights are on display in the building's rotunda. Call at least three weeks in advance to arrange a behind-the-scenes tour. ⊠ *Constitution Ave. between 7th and 9th Sts. NW,* ☎ *202/501–5000 or 202/501–5205 for tours.* 🎟 *Free.* ☉ *Apr.–Labor Day, daily 10–9; Sept.–Mar., daily 10–5:30; tours weekdays at 10:15 and 1:15. Metro: Archives/Navy Memorial.*

National Museum of American Art. The first floor of the National Museum of American Art, which is in the ☞ **Old Patent Office Building**, has displays of early American art and art of the West, as well as a gallery of painted miniatures. Be sure to see *The Throne of the Third Heaven of the Nations' Millennium General Assembly,* by James Hampton. Discarded materials, such as chairs, bottles, and light bulbs, are sheathed in aluminum and gold foil in this strange and moving work of religious art. On the second floor are works by the American impressionists, including Childe Hassam and Cassatt, sculptures by Hiram Powers, and massive landscapes by Albert Bierstadt and Thomas Moran. The third floor is filled with modern art, including works by Leon Kroll and Edward Hopper that were commissioned during the '30s by the federal government. The Lincoln Gallery—site of the receiving line at Abraham Lincoln's 1865 inaugural ball—has been restored to its original appearance and displays 20th-century art. ✉ *8th and G Sts. NW,* ☎ *202/357–2700 or 202/357–1729 TDD.* 🎫 *Free.* ⊙ *Daily 10–5:30. Metro: Gallery Place/Chinatown.*

❷ **National Museum of Women in the Arts.** Works by female artists from the Renaissance to the present are showcased at one of the larger non-Smithsonian museums. The beautifully restored 1907 Renaissance Revival building was designed by Waddy Wood; ironically, it was once a men-only Masonic temple. In addition to displaying traveling shows, the museum has a permanent collection that includes paintings, drawings, sculpture, prints, and photographs by such artists as Georgia O'Keeffe, Mary Cassatt, Élisabeth Vigée-Lebrun, Frida Kahlo, and Judy Chicago. ✉ *1250 New York Ave. NW,* ☎ *202/783–5000.* 🎫 *Suggested donation $3.* ⊙ *Mon.–Sat. 10–5, Sun. noon–5. Metro: Metro Center.*

National Portrait Gallery. This museum is in the ☞ **Old Patent Office Building** along with the ☞ **National Museum of American Art.** The best place to start a circuit of the Portrait Gallery is on the restored third floor. The mezzanine level of the wonderfully busy room features a **Civil War exhibition,** with portraits, photographs, and lithographs of such wartime personalities as Julia Ward Howe, Frederick Douglass, Ulysses S. Grant, and Robert E. Lee. There are also life casts of Abraham Lincoln's hands and face. The restored Renaissance-style gallery has colorful tile flooring and a stained-glass skylight. Highlights of the Portrait Gallery's second floor include the **Hall of Presidents** (featuring a portrait or sculpture of each chief executive) and the George Washington "Lansdowne" portrait. The first floor features portraits of well-known American athletes and performers. *Time* magazine gave the museum its collection of Person of the Year covers and many other photos and paintings that the magazine has commissioned over the years. Parts of this collection are periodically on display. ⊠ *8th and F Sts. NW,* ☎ *202/357–2700 or 202/357–1729 TDD.* ⊠ *Free.* ☼ *Daily 10–5:30. Metro: Gallery Place/Chinatown.*

❹ **Old Patent Office Building.** Two Smithsonian museums now share the Old Patent Office Building. The ☞ **National Portrait Gallery** is on the south side; the ☞ **National Museum of American Art** is on the north. Construction on the south wing, which was designed by Washington Monument architect Robert Mills, started in 1836. When the huge Greek Revival quadrangle was completed in 1867, it was the largest building in the country. Many of its rooms housed glass display cabinets filled with the models that inventors were required to submit with their patent applications. During the Civil War, the Patent Office, like many other buildings in the city, was turned into a hospital. Among those caring for the wounded here were Clara Barton and Walt Whitman. The Smithsonian opened it to the public in 1968. ⊠ *G St. between 7th and 9th Sts.*

☾ ❸ **Old Post Office Building.** When it was completed in 1899, this Romanesque structure on Federal Triangle was the largest government building in the District, the first with a clock tower, and the first with an electric power plant. Despite these innovations, it earned the sobriquet "old" after only 18 years, when a new District post office was constructed near Union Station. Park service rangers who work at the Old Post Office consider the observation deck in the **clock tower** to be one of Washington's best-kept secrets. Although not as tall as the Washington Monument, it offers nearly as impressive a view. Even better, it's usually not as crowded; the windows are bigger, and—unlike the monument's windows—they're open, allowing cool breezes to waft through. (The tour is about 15 minutes long.) ⊠ *Pennsylvania Ave. and 12th St. NW,* ☎ *202/606–8691 tower, 202/289–4224 pavilion.* 🖃 *Free.* ☉ *Tower Easter– Labor Day, daily 8 AM–11 PM (last tour 10:45); Sept.–Mar., daily 8–6 (last tour 5:45). Metro: Federal Triangle.*

Ronald Reagan Building and International Trade Center. This new, $818 million, 3.1-million-square-ft colossus is the largest federal building to be constructed in the Washington area since the Pentagon. A blend of classical and modern architecture, the Indiana limestone structure with its huge, domed corner piece, replaced what for 50 years had been a huge parking lot, an eyesore that interrupted the flow of the buildings of Federal Triangle. At present, the Reagan building is home to the Environmental Protection Agency, an odd irony considering the building's namesake's dislike for that agency. Future plans include a food court, international trade facilities, and public spaces. ⊠ *1300 Pennsylvania Ave. NW. Metro: Federal Triangle.*

Georgetown

The area that would come to be known as George (after George II), then George Towne and, finally, Georgetown, was part of Maryland when it was settled in the early 1700s by Scottish immigrants. Georgetown's position at the farthest point up the Potomac accessible by boat made it an ideal transit and inspection point for farmers who grew tobacco in Maryland's interior. In 1789 the state granted the town a charter, but two years later Georgetown—along with Alexandria, its counterpart in Virginia—was included by George Washington in the Territory of Columbia, site of the new capital.

Tobacco eventually became a less important commodity, and Georgetown became a milling center, using water power from the Potomac. When the Chesapeake & Ohio (C&O) Canal was completed in 1850, the city intensified its milling operations and became the eastern end of a waterway that stretched 184 mi to the west. The canal took up some of the slack when Georgetown's harbor began to fill with silt and the port lost business to Alexandria and Baltimore, but the canal never became the success it was meant to be. In the years that followed, Georgetown was a far cry from the fashionable spot it is today. Clustered near the water were a foundry, a fish market, paper and cotton mills, and a power station for the city's streetcar system. It still had its Georgian, Federal, and Victorian homes, though, and when the New Deal and World War II brought a flood of newcomers to Washington, Georgetown's tree-shaded streets and handsome brick houses were rediscovered. Pushed out in the process were Georgetown's blacks, most of whom rented the houses they lived in.

Washington has filled in around Georgetown over the years, but the former tobacco port retains an air of aloofness. Its narrow streets, which refuse to conform to Pierre L'Enfant's plan for the Federal City, make up the capital's wealthiest neighborhood and are the nucleus of its nightlife. The lack of a Metro station in Georgetown means you'll have to take a bus or taxi or walk to this part of Washington. It's about a 15-minute walk from the Dupont Circle or Foggy Bottom Metro station. (If you'd rather take a bus, the G2 Georgetown University bus goes from Dupont Circle west along P Street. The 34 and 36 Friendship Heights buses leave from 22nd and Pennsylvania and deposit you at 31st and M.)

Numbers in the margin correspond to numbers on the Georgetown map; these indicate a suggested path for sightseeing.

Sights to See

① **C&O Canal.** This waterway kept Georgetown open to shipping after its harbor had filled with silt. George Washington was one of the first to advance the idea of a canal linking the Potomac with the Ohio River across the Appalachians. Work started on the C&O Canal in 1828, and when it opened in 1850, its 74 locks linked Georgetown with Cumberland, Maryland, 184 mi to the northwest. Lumber, coal, iron, wheat, and flour moved up and down the canal, but it was never as successful as its planners had hoped it

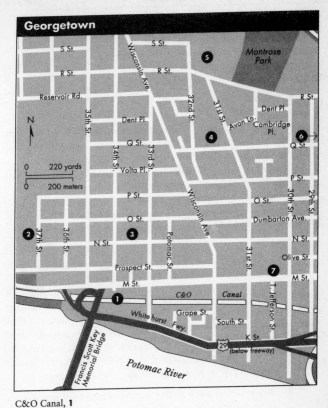

Georgetown

S St.

S St.

R St.

R St.

Montrose
Park

Reservoir Rd.

Dent Pl.

R St.

Wisconsin Ave.

32nd St.

31st St.

Avon Ln.

Cambridge
Pl.

Dent Pl.

N

35th St.

34th St.

33rd St.

Q St.

Q St.

Volta Pl.

0   220 yards

0   200 meters

P St.

O St.

N St.

Wisconsin Ave.

O St.

Dumbarton Ave.

P St.

30th St.

29th St.

37th St.

36th St.

Prospect St.

Potomac St.

31st St.

N St.

Olive St.

M St.

M St.

T. Jefferson St.

C&O   Canal

White hurst Fwy.

Grape St.

South St.

K St.

29 (below freeway)

Francis Scott Key
Memorial Bridge

Potomac River

C&O Canal, **1**

Cox's Row, **3**

Dumbarton
House, **6**

Dumbarton
Oaks, **5**

Georgetown
University, **2**

Old Stone
House, **7**

Tudor Place, **4**

would be. Many of the bridges spanning the canal in Georgetown were too low to allow anything other than fully loaded barges to pass underneath, and competition from the Baltimore & Ohio Railroad eventually spelled an end to profitability. Today the canal is a part of the National Park System, and walkers follow the towpath once used by mules while canoeists paddle the canal's calm waters. ⊠ *1057 Thomas Jefferson St. NW,* ☎ *202/653–5190.* 🎟 *Barge trip $7.50.* ☉ *Barge trips: Mid-Apr.–June 14 and Sept. 9–Nov. 1, Wed.–Fri. 11 and 2:30; Sat.–Sun. 11, 1, 2:30 and 4. June 17–Sept. 7, Wed.–Fri 11, 1, and 2:30; Sat.– Sun. 11, 1, 2:30, and 4.* ⊠ *11710 MacArthur Blvd., Potomac, MD,* ☎ *301/299–3613.* 🎟 *Barge trip $7.50.* ☉ *Barge trips: Mid-Apr.–June 14 and Sept. 9–Nov.1, Wed.– Fri. 2:30; Sat.–Sun. 11, 1, 2:30, and 4. June 17–Sept. 7, Wed.–Fri 11, 1, and 2:30; Sat.–Sun. 11, 1, 2:30, and 4.*

❸ Cox's Row. Architecture buffs, especially those interested in Federal and Victorian houses, enjoy wandering along the redbrick sidewalks of upper Georgetown. To get a representative taste of the houses in the area, walk along the 3300 block of N Street. The group of five Federal houses between 3339 and 3327 N Street is known collectively as Cox's Row, after John Cox, a former mayor of Georgetown, who built them in 1817. The flat-front, redbrick Federal house at 3307 N Street was the home of then-Senator John F. Kennedy and his family before the White House beckoned.

❻ Dumbarton House. Its symmetry and the two curved wings on its north side make Dumbarton, built around 1800, a distinctive example of Georgian architecture. Eight rooms inside Dumbarton House have been restored to Colonial splendor, with period furnishings such as mahogany American Chippendale chairs, hallmark silver, Persian rugs, and a breakfront cabinet filled with rare books. ⊠ *2715 Q St. NW,* ☎ *202/337–2288.* 🎟 *Suggested donation $3.* ☉ *Tues.–Sat. 10–12:15.*

❺ Dumbarton Oaks. In 1944 one of the most important events of the 20th century took place in Dumbarton Oaks, when representatives of the United States, Great Britain, China, and the Soviet Union met in the music room here to lay the groundwork for the United Nations. Career diplomat

Robert Woods Bliss and his wife, Mildred, bought the property in 1920 and set about taming the sprawling grounds and removing 19th-century additions that had marred the Federal lines of the 1801 mansion. In 1940 the Blisses conveyed the estate to Harvard University, which maintains world-renowned collections of Byzantine and pre-Columbian art there. Both are small but choice, reflecting the enormous skill and creativity going on at roughly the same time on two sides of the Atlantic.

Dumbarton Oaks's 10 acres of formal gardens, with a stunning collection of terraces, geometric gardens, tree-shaded brick walks, fountains, arbors, and pools, incorporate elements of traditional English, Italian, and French land-scaping styles. Plenty of well-positioned benches make this a good place for resting weary feet, too. Enter via R Street. ⊠ *Art collections, 1703 32nd St. NW,* ☎ *202/339–6401 or 202/339–6400;* ⊠ *Gardens, 31st and R Sts. NW.* 🖭 *Art collections, suggested donation $1; gardens Apr.–Oct. $4, Nov.–Mar. free.* ☉ *Art collections Tues.–Sun. 2–5; gardens Apr.–Oct., daily 2–6; Nov.–Mar., daily 2–5.*

② **Georgetown University.** Founded in 1789 by John Carroll, first American bishop and first archbishop of Baltimore, Georgetown is the oldest Jesuit school in the country. About 12,000 students attend Georgetown, known now as much for its perennially successful basketball team as for its fine programs in law, medicine, foreign service, and the liberal arts. ⊠ *37th and O Sts.,* ☎ *202/687–5055.*

⑦ **Old Stone House.** What was early American life like? Here's the capital's oldest window into the past. Work on this field-stone house, thought to be Washington's only surviving pre-Revolutionary building, was begun in 1764 by a cabinetmaker named Christopher Layman. The house, now a museum, was used as both a residence and a place of busi-ness by a succession of occupants. Five of the house's rooms are furnished with the simple sturdy artifacts—plain tables, spinning wheels, etc.—of 18th-century middle-class life. The National Park Service maintains the house and its lovely gardens. ⊠ *3051 M St. NW,* ☎ *202/426–6851.* 🖭 *Free.* ☉ *Memorial Day–Labor Day, daily 9–5; Labor Day–Memorial Day, Wed.–Sun. 9–5.*

❹ **Tudor Place.** Stop at Q Street between 31st and 32nd streets; look through the trees to the north, at the top of a sloping lawn; and you'll see the neoclassical Tudor Place, designed by Capitol architect Dr. William Thornton and completed in 1816. On a house tour you'll see chairs that belonged to George Washington; Francis Scott Key's desk; and spurs of members of the Peter family, who were killed in the Civil War. The house was built for Thomas Peter, son of Georgetown's first mayor, and his wife, Martha Custis, Martha Washington's granddaughter. The yellow stucco house is interesting for its architecture—especially the dramatic, two-story domed portico on the south side—but its familial heritage is even more remarkable: Tudor Place stayed in the same family for 178 years, until 1983, when Armistead Peter III died. Before his death, Peter established a foundation to restore the house and open it to the public. Tour reservations are advised. ⊠ *1644 31st St. NW,* ☎ *202/965-0400.* 🎫 *Suggested donation $6.* ⊙ *House tours Tues.– Fri. at 10, 11:30, 1, and 2:30; Sat. hourly 10–4 (last tour at 3); garden open Mon.–Sat. 10–4 (also Sun. noon–4 Apr.– May and Sept.–Oct.).*

Dupont Circle

Originally known as Pacific Circle, this hub was the westernmost circle in Pierre L'Enfant's original design for the Federal City. The name was changed in 1884, when Congress authorized construction of a bronze statue honoring Civil War hero Admiral Samuel F. Dupont. The statue fell into disrepair, and Dupont's family—who had never liked it anyway—replaced it in 1921. The marble fountain—with allegorical figures Sea, Stars, and Wind—that stands in its place was created by Daniel Chester French, the sculptor of Lincoln's statue in the Lincoln Memorial. Since a half dozen streets converge on Dupont Circle, the buildings around it are, for the most part, wedge-shape and set on oddly shaped plots of land like massive slices of pie.

With a small, handsome park and a splashing fountain in the center, Dupont Circle is more than a deserted island around which traffic flows; the activity spills over into the surrounding streets, one of the liveliest, most vibrant neighborhoods in DC. Stores and clubs catering to the neighborhood's large gay community are abundant.

Numbers in the margin correspond to numbers on the Dupont Circle and Foggy Bottom map; these indicate a suggested path for sightseeing.

Sights to See

❷ **Anderson House.** Larz Anderson was a diplomat whose career included postings to Japan and Belgium. Anderson and his heiress wife, Isabel, toured the world, picking up objects that struck their fancy. They filled their residence, which was constructed in 1905, with the booty of their travels, including choir stalls from an Italian Renaissance church, Flemish tapestries, and a large—if spotty—collection of Asian art. All this remains in the house for you to see.

In accordance with Anderson's wishes, the building also serves as the headquarters of a group to which he belonged: the **Society of the Cincinnati.** The oldest patriotic organization in the country, the society was formed in 1783 by a group of officers who had served with George Washington during the Revolutionary War. The group took the name Cincinnati from Cincinnatus, a distinguished Roman who, circa 500 BC, led an army against Rome's enemies and later quelled civil disturbances in the city. Today's members are direct descendants of those American revolutionaries. The house is often used by the federal government to entertain visiting dignitaries. Amid the glitz, glamour, beauty, and patriotic spectacle of the mansion are two delightful painted panels in the solarium that depict the Andersons' favorite motor-car sight-seeing routes around Washington. ✉ *2118 Massachusetts Ave. NW,* ☎ *202/785–2040.* ✉ *Free.* ☉ *Tues.–Sat. 1–4. Metro: Dupont Circle.*

❸ **Bison Bridge.** Tour guides at the Smithsonian's Museum of Natural History are quick to remind you that America never had buffalo; the big shaggy animals that roamed the plains were bison. Though many maps and guidebooks call this the Buffalo Bridge, the four bronze statues by A. Phimister Proctor are of bison. Officially called the **Dumbarton Bridge,** the structure stretches across Rock Creek Park into Georgetown. ✉ *23rd and Q Sts. NW. Metro: Dupont Circle.*

Dupont Circle and Foggy Bottom

KEY

AE American Express Office

Anderson
House, **2**

Bison Bridge, **3**

B'nai B'rith
Klutznick
Museum, **9**

Council
House, **10**

Department
of State, **15**

Federal
Reserve
Building, **16**

George
Washington
University, **13**

Heurich House
Museum, **1**

Metropolitan
African
Methodist
Episcopal
Church, **11**

National
Geographic
Society, **12**

National
Museum of
American
Jewish Military
History, **7**

Phillips
Collection, **6**

St. Matthew's
Cathedral, **8**

Textile
Museum, **5**

Watergate, **14**

Woodrow
Wilson
House, **4**

9 **B'nai B'rith Klutznick Museum.** Devoted to the history of Jewish people, this museum's permanent exhibits span 20 centuries and highlight Jewish festivals and rituals. A wide variety of Jewish decorative art, adorning such items as spice boxes and Torah covers, is on display. Changing exhibits highlight the work of contemporary Jewish artists. ⊠ *1640 Rhode Island Ave. NW,* ☎ *202/857–6583.* 🎫 *Suggested donation $2.* ☉ *Sun.–Fri. 10–5. Metro: Dupont Circle or Farragut North.*

10 **Council House.** Exhibits in this museum focus on the achievements of black women, including Mary McLeod Bethune, who founded Florida's Bethune-Cookman College, established the National Council of Negro Women, and served as an adviser to President Franklin D. Roosevelt. ⊠ *1318 Vermont Ave. NW,* ☎ *202/673–2402.* 🎫 *Free.* ☉ *Mon.– Sat. 10–4. Metro: McPherson Square.*

1 **Heurich House Museum.** Currently housing the **Historical Society of Washington**, this opulent Romanesque Revival was the home of Christian Heurich, a German orphan who made his fortune in this country in the beer business. Heurich's brewery was in Foggy Bottom, where the Kennedy Center stands today. After Heurich's widow died, in 1955, the house was turned over to the historical society and today houses a research library and museum. Most of the furnishings in the house were owned and used by the Heurichs. The interior is an eclectic Victorian treasure trove of plaster detailing, carved wooden doors, and painted ceilings. The docents who give these tours are adept at answering questions about other Washington landmarks. ⊠ *1307 New Hampshire Ave. NW,* ☎ *202/785–2068.* 🎫 *$3.* ☉ *Wed.–Sat. 10–4. Metro: Dupont Circle.*

11 **Metropolitan African Methodist Episcopal Church.** Completed in 1886, the Gothic-style Metropolitan African Methodist Episcopal Church became one of the most influential black churches in the city. Abolitionist orator Frederick Douglass worshiped here, and Bill Clinton chose the church as the setting for his inaugural prayer service. ⊠ *1518 M St. NW,* ☎ *202/331–1426. Metro: Farragut North.*

🕑 ⑫ **National Geographic Society.** The society, founded in 1888, is best known for its yellow-border magazine, found in doctor's offices, family rooms, and attics across the country. The society has sponsored numerous expeditions throughout its 100-year history, including those of Admirals Peary and Byrd and underwater explorer Jacques Cousteau. Interactive **Explorers Hall,** entered from 17th Street, is the magazine come to life. You can experience everything from a minitornado to video "touch-screens" that explain geographic concepts. The most dramatic events take place in Earth Station One, a 72-seat amphitheater that sends the audience on a journey around the world. ⊠ *17th and M Sts.,* ☎ *202/857–7588 or 202/ 857–7689 group tours.* ⊠ *Free.* ☉ *Mon.–Sat. 9–5, Sun. 10–5. Metro: Farragut North.*

⑦ **National Museum of American Jewish Military History.** The museum's focus is on American Jews who have served in every war the nation has fought. On display are weapons, uniforms, medals, recruitment posters, and other military memorabilia. The few specifically religious items—a camouflage yarmulke, rabbinical supplies fashioned from shell casings and parachute silk—underscore the strange demands placed on religion during war. ⊠ *1811 R St. NW,* ☎ *202/265–6280.* ⊠ *Free.* ☉ *Weekdays 9–5, Sun. 1–5. Metro: Dupont Circle.*

⑥ **Phillips Collection.** The first permanent museum of modern art in the country, the masterpiece-filled Phillips Collection is unique both in origin and content. In 1918 Duncan Phillips, grandson of a founder of the Jones and Laughlin Steel Company, started to collect art for a museum that would stand as a memorial to his father and brother, who had died within 13 months of each other. Three years later what was first called the Phillips Memorial Gallery opened in two rooms of this Georgian Revival home near Dupont Circle. Holdings include works by Georges Braque, Paul Cézanne, Paul Klee, Henri Matisse, John Henry Twachtman, and the largest museum collection in the country of the work of Pierre Bonnard. The exhibits change regularly. ⊠ *1600 21st St. NW,* ☎ *202/387–2151.* ⊠ *$6.50; Thurs. night $5.* ☉ *Tues.–Wed. and Fri.–Sat. 10–5; Thurs. 10– 8:30; Sun. noon–7 (noon–5 June–Aug.); tour Wed. and*

Sat. at 2; gallery talks 1st and 3rd Thurs. of month at 12:30. Metro: Dupont Circle.

8 **St. Matthew's Cathedral.** St. Matthew's is the seat of Washington's Catholic archbishop. John F. Kennedy frequently worshiped in this Renaissance-style church, and in 1963 his funeral mass was held within its richly decorated walls. ✉ *1725 Rhode Island Ave. NW,* ☎ *202/347–3215.* 🎫 *Free.* ☉ *Weekdays and Sun. 7–6:30, Sat. 8–6:30; tour usually Sun. at 2:30. Metro: Farragut North.*

5 **Textile Museum.** In the 1890s, founder George Hewitt Myers purchased his first Oriental rug for his dorm room at Yale. An heir to the Bristol-Myers fortune, Myers and his wife lived two houses down from Woodrow Wilson, at 2310 S Street, in a home designed by John Russell Pope, architect of the National Archives and the Jefferson Memorial. Myers bought the Waddy Wood–designed house next door, at No. 2320, and opened his museum to the public in 1925. Today the collection includes more than 15,500 rugs and textiles and includes Coptic and pre-Columbian textiles, Kashmir embroidery, and Turkman tribal rugs. ✉ *2320 S St. NW,* ☎ *202/667–0441.* 🎫 *Suggested donation $5.* ☉ *Mon.–Sat. 10–5, Sun. 1–5; highlight tour Sept.– May, Wed. and weekends at 2. Metro: Dupont Circle.*

4 **Woodrow Wilson House.** Wilson is the only president who stayed in DC after leaving the White House. (He's also the only president buried in the city, inside the National Cathedral.) He and his second wife, Edith Bolling Wilson, retired in 1920 to this Georgian Revival. President Wilson suffered a stroke toward the end of his second term, in 1919, and he lived out the last few years of his life on this quiet street. Wilson died in 1924. Edith survived him by 37 years. After she died in 1961, the house and its contents were bequeathed to the National Trust for Historic Preservation. On view inside are such items as a Gobelins tapestry, a baseball signed by King George V, and the shell casing from the first shot fired by U.S. forces in World War I. The house also contains memorabilia related to the history of the short-lived League of Nations, including the colorful flag Wilson hoped would be adopted by that organization. ✉ *2340 S St. NW,* ☎ *202/387–4062.* 🎫 *$5.* ☉ *Tues.–Sun. 10–4. Metro: Dupont Circle.*

Foggy Bottom

The Foggy Bottom area of Washington—bordered roughly by the Potomac and Rock Creek to the west, 20th Street to the east, Pennsylvania Avenue to the north, and Constitution Avenue to the south—has three main claims to fame: the State Department, the Kennedy Center, and George Washington University. In 1763 a German immigrant named Jacob Funk purchased this land, and a community called Funkstown sprang up on the Potomac. This nickname is only slightly less amusing than the present one, an appellation derived from the wharves, breweries, lime kilns, and glassworks that were near the water. Smoke from these factories combined with the swampy air of the low-lying ground to produce a permanent fog along the waterfront.

The smoke-belching factories ensured work for the hundreds of German and Irish immigrants who settled in Foggy Bottom in the 19th century. By the 1930s, however, industry was on the way out, and Foggy Bottom had become a poor part of Washington. The opening of the State Department headquarters in 1947 reawakened middle-class interest in the neighborhood's modest row houses. Many of them are now gone, and Foggy Bottom today suffers from a split personality as tiny, one-room-wide row houses sit next to large, mixed-use developments.

Although the Foggy Bottom neighborhood has its own Metro stop, many attractions are a considerable distance away. If you don't relish long walks or time is limited, check the Foggy Bottom map to see if you need to make alternate travel arrangements to visit specific sights.

Numbers in the margin correspond to numbers on the Dupont Circle and Foggy Bottom map; these indicate a suggested path for sightseeing.

Sights to See

⑮ Department of State. The foreign policy of the United States is formulated and administered by battalions of brainy analysts in the huge Department of State building (often referred to as the State Department), which also serves as the headquarters of the United States Diplomatic Corps. All is presided over by the secretary of state, who is fourth in line for the presidency (after the vice president, speaker of the House, and president *pro tempore* of the Senate, respectively) should the president be unable to serve. On the top floor are the opulent **Diplomatic Reception Rooms,** decorated in the manner of great halls of Europe, and the rooms of Colonial American plantations. The museum-quality furnishings include a Philadelphia highboy, a Paul Revere bowl, and the desk on which the Treaty of Paris was signed. Make sure you register for a tour well ahead of your visit. ✉ *23rd and C Sts. NW,* ☎ *202/647–3241 or 202/736–4474 TDD.* 🎟 *Free.* ☽ *Tours weekdays at 9:30, 10:30, and 2:45. Metro: Foggy Bottom.*

⑯ Federal Reserve Building. Whether or not interest rates are raised or lowered in attempts to control the economy is decided in this imposing marble edifice, whose bronze entryway is topped by a massive eagle. Designed by Folger Library architect Paul Cret, "the Fed" is on Constitution Avenue between 21st and 20th streets. It seems to say, "Your money's safe with us." Even so, there isn't any money here. Ft. Knox holds most of the government's gold. The stolid Fed has a varied collection of art and four special art exhibitions every year. A 45-minute tour includes a film that attempts to explain exactly what it is that the Fed does. ✉ *Enter on C St. between 20th and 21st Sts.,* ☎ *202/452–3000, 202/452–3149 building tours, or 202/452–3686 art tours.* 🎟 *Free.* ☽ *Weekdays 11–2 during art exhibitions (tours of permanent art collection by appointment only); building tour Thurs. at 2:30. Metro: Foggy Bottom.*

⑬ George Washington University. George Washington had always hoped the capital would be home to a world-class university. He even left 50 shares of stock in the Patowmack Canal Co. to endow it. Congress never acted upon his wishes, however, and it wasn't until 1822 that a university eventually named after the first president began to take shape. The private Columbian College in the District of Columbia opened that year with the aim of training students for the Baptist ministry. In 1904 the university shed its Baptist connections and changed its name to George Washington University. In 1912 it moved to its present location and since that time has become the second largest landholder in the District (after the federal government). Alumni include J. Edgar Hoover to Jacqueline Bouvier. ✉ *Downtown campus covers much of Foggy Bottom south of Pennsylvania Avenue between 19th and 24th Sts.* ☎ *202/994–1000. Metro: Foggy Bottom.*

⓮ Watergate. Thanks to the events that took place on the night of June 17, 1972, the Watergate is possibly the world's most notorious apartment-office complex. As Nixon aides E. Howard Hunt Jr. and G. Gordon Liddy sat in the Howard Johnson Motor Lodge across the street, five of their men were caught trying to bug the Democratic National Committee, headquartered on the building's sixth floor, in an attempt to subvert the democratic process on behalf of the then president of the United States. A marketing company occupies the space today. ✉ *2600 Virginia Ave. Metro: Foggy Bottom.*

Adams-Morgan/Woodley Park

Cleveland Park, a tree-shaded neighborhood in northwest Washington, owes its name to onetime summer resident Grover Cleveland, who established a summer White House on Newark Street between 35th and 36th streets. Many prominent Washingtonians followed suit. Today the neighborhood's attractive houses and suburban character are popular with Washington professionals.

Southeast of Cleveland Park, Adams-Morgan (roughly, the blocks north of Florida Avenue, between Connecticut Avenue and 16th Street NW) is Washington's most ethnically diverse neighborhood. And as is so often the case, that means it's one of Washington's most interesting areas—home to a United Nations of cuisines, offbeat shops, and funky bars and clubs. As in Georgetown, there's no Metro stop in Adams-Morgan. It's a 15-minute walk from the Woodley Park/Zoo Metro station: Walk south on Connecticut, then turn left on Calvert Street, and cross over Rock Creek Park on the Duke Ellington Bridge. Or you can get off at the Dupont Circle Metro stop and walk east to (and turn left onto) 18th Street. The heart of Adams-Morgan is at the crossroads of Adams Mill Road, Columbia Road, and 18th Street.

Numbers in the text correspond to numbers on the Adams-Morgan/Woodley Park map; these indicate a suggested path for sightseeing.

Sights to See

❹ District of Columbia Arts Center. A combination art gallery and performance space, the DCAC exhibits cutting-edge work of local artists and is the host of offbeat plays and performance art. ✉ *2438 18th St. NW,* ☎ *202/462–7833.* 🎟 *Gallery free, performance costs vary.* ☉ *Wed.–Thurs. 2–6, Fri.–Sun. 2–10, and during performances (generally Thurs.–Sun. 7 PM–midnight).*

❶ Hillwood Museum and Gardens. Hillwood House, cereal heiress Marjorie Merriweather Post's 40-room Georgian mansion, contains a large collection of 18th- and 19th-century French and Russian decorative art. The grounds are composed of formal French and Japanese gardens and paths that wind through azaleas, laurels, and rhododendrons. The house and gardens are closed for renovation until the spring of 2000, but lecture, music, and travel programs will continue thereafter. ✉ *4155 Linnean Ave. NW,* ☎ *202/686–5807 or 202/686–8500.* 🎟 *House and grounds $10; grounds only $2.* ☉ *House tours Mar.–Jan., Tues.–Sat. 9:30–3; grounds Mar.–Jan., Tues.–Sat. 9–5. Metro: Van Ness/UDC.*

❷ Kennedy-Warren. The apartment house is a superb example of Art Deco architecture, with period detailing like decorative aluminum panels and a streamlined entryway, stone griffins under the pyramidal copper roof, and stylized carved eagles flanking the driveways. ✉ *3133 Connecticut Ave. NW. Metro: Cleveland Park.*

❼ Meridian House and the White-Meyer House. Meridian International Center, a nonprofit institution promoting international understanding, owns two handsome mansions designed by John Russell Pope. The 30-room Meridian House was built in 1920 by Irwin Boyle Laughlin, scion of a Pittsburgh steel family and former ambassador to Spain. The Louis XVI–style home features parquet floors, ornamental iron grillwork, period furniture, tapestries, and a garden planted with European linden trees. Next door is the Georgian-style house built for Henry White (former am-

Adams-Morgan/Woodley Park

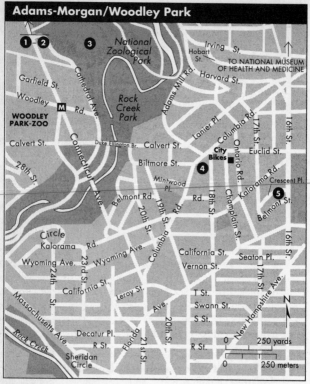

District of
Columbia Arts
Center, **4**

Hillwood
Museum and
Gardens, **1**

Kennedy-
Warren, **2**

Meridian House
and the
White-Meyer
House, **5**

National
Zoological
Park, **3**

bassador to France) that was later the home of the Meyer family, publishers of the *Washington Post*. The first floors of both houses are open to the public and are the scene of periodic art exhibits with an international flavor. ✉ *1630 and 1624 Crescent Pl. NW,* ☎ *202/667–6800.* ✇ *Free.* ☉ *Wed.–Sun. 2–5.*

🕊 ❸ **National Zoological Park.** Part of the Smithsonian Institution, the National Zoo is one of the foremost zoos in the world. Created by an Act of Congress in 1889, the 163-acre park was designed by landscape architect Frederick Law Olmsted, who designed the U.S. Capitol grounds. Innovative compounds show many animals in naturalistic settings, including the Great Flight Cage—a walk-in aviary in which birds fly unrestricted from May to October (they're moved indoors during the colder months). Zoolab, the Reptile Discovery Center, and the Bird Resource Center all offer activities that teach young visitors about biology. The most ambitious addition to the zoo is Amazonia, a reproduction of a South American rain-forest ecosystem. Fish swim behind glass walls, while overhead, monkeys and birds flit from tree to tree. The temperature is a constant 85°F, with 85% humidity. The Cheetah Conservation Area is a grassy compound that's home to a family of the world's fastest cats. ✉ *3000 block of Connecticut Ave. NW,* ☎ *202/ 673–4800 or 202/673–4717.* ✇ *Free.* ☉ *May 1–Sept. 15, grounds daily 6 AM–8 PM, animal buildings daily 10–6 (may be open later in summer); Sept. 16–Apr. 30, grounds daily 6–6, animal buildings daily 10–4:30. Metro: Cleveland Park or Woodley Park/Zoo.*

Woodley Park. The stretch of Connecticut Avenue south of the ☞ **National Zoological Park** is bordered by apartment buildings. Passing Cathedral Avenue (the first cross street south of the zoo), you enter a part of town known as Woodley Park. Like Cleveland Park to the north, Woodley Park grew as the streetcar advanced into this part of Washington. In 1800 Philip Barton Key, uncle of Francis Scott Key, built **Woodley**, a Georgian mansion on Cathedral Avenue between 29th and 31st streets. The white stucco mansion was the summer home of four presidents: Van Buren, Tyler, Buchanan, and Cleveland. It's now owned by the private Maret School. *Metro: Woodley Park/Zoo.*

Around Washington, DC

The environs of Washington are dotted with worthwhile attractions. Three sights in Arlington—each linked to the military—that should be a part of any complete visit to the nation's capital: Arlington National Cemetery, the U.S. Marine Corps War Memorial, and the Pentagon. South of Arlington and a short Metro ride from Washington, Old Town Alexandria provides a change of pace from the hustle-and-bustle of the District. The city's colorful history is still alive in restored 18th- and 19th-century homes, churches, and taverns; on the cobbled streets; and on the revitalized waterfront, where clipper ships dock and artisans display their wares. The quickest way to get to Old Town is to take the Metro to the King Street stop. If you're driving you can take either the George Washington Memorial Parkway or Jefferson Davis Highway (Route 1) south from Arlington.

Sights to See

Arlington National Cemetery. Some 250,000 American war dead, as well as many notable Americans (among them Presidents William Howard Taft and John F. Kennedy, General John Pershing, and Admiral Robert E. Peary), are interred in these 612 acres across the Potomac River from Washington, established as the nation's cemetery in 1864. While you're at Arlington you'll probably hear the clear, doleful sound of a trumpet playing taps or the sharp reports of a gun salute. Approximately 15 funerals are held daily. Although not the largest cemetery in the country, Arlington is certainly the best known, a place where you can trace America's history through the aftermath of its battles.

To get to the cemetery, you can take the Metro, travel on a Tourmobile bus, or walk across Memorial Bridge from the District (southwest of the Lincoln Memorial). If you're driving, there's a large paid parking lot at the skylit visitor center on Memorial Drive. Stop at the center for a free brochure with a detailed map of the cemetery. If you're looking for a specific grave, the staff will help you find it. Tourmobile tour buses leave from just outside the visitor center April 1–September 30, daily 8:30–6:30, and October 1–March 31, daily 8:30–4:30. You can buy tickets here for the 40-minute tour of the cemetery, which includes stops at the ☞ **Kennedy graves,** the ☞ **Tomb of the Unknowns,** and Arlington House. Touring the cemetery on foot means a fair bit of hiking, but if you decide to walk, head west from the visitor center on Roosevelt Drive and then turn right on Weeks Drive. ⊠ *West end of Memorial Bridge, Arlington, VA,* ☎ *703/607–8052 or 703/697–2131 to locate a grave.* ▣ *Cemetery free; tours $4.* ☉ *Apr.–Sept., daily 8–7; Oct.–Mar., daily 8–5.*

Boyhood Home of Robert E. Lee. The childhood home in Alexandria of the commander in chief of the Confederate forces during the Civil War is a fine example of a 19th-century town house with Federal architecture and antique furnishings and paintings. ⊠ *607 Oronoco St.,* ☎ *703/ 548–8454.* ▣ *$4.* ☉ *Mon.–Sat. 10–4, Sun. 1–4; closed Dec. 15–Feb. 1 except on Sun. closest to Jan. 19 for Lee's birthday celebration; occasionally closed weekends for private events.*

Gadsby's Tavern Museum. This museum is housed in the old City Tavern and Hotel, which was a center of political and social life in the late 18th century. George Washington attended birthday celebrations in the ballroom here. A tour takes you through the taproom, dining room, assembly room, ball room, and communal bedrooms. ⊠ *134 N. Royal St., Alexandria,* ☎ *703/838–4242.* ▣ *$4.* ☉ *Oct.– Mar., Tues.–Sat. 11–4, Sun. 1–4 (last tour 3:15); Apr.– Sept., Tues.–Sat. 10–5, Sun. 1–5 (last tour 4:15); tours 15 min before and 15 min after the hr.*

Kennedy graves. A highlight of the Arlington National Cemetery is a visit to the graves of John F. Kennedy and members of his family, just west of the visitor center. JFK is buried under an eternal flame near two of his children, who died in infancy, and his wife, Jacqueline Bouvier Kennedy Onassis. Across from them is a low wall engraved with quotations from Kennedy's inaugural address. JFK's grave was opened to the public in 1967 and since that time has become the most-visited grave site in the country.

Nearby, marked by a simple white cross, is the grave of his brother, Robert Kennedy. ⊠ *Sheridan and Weeks Drs.*

Newseum. At the first and only museum dedicated to the business of news, you can relive recent history's defining moments; learn how journalism evolved; try your hand at reporting, anchoring, and weathercasting; see artifacts like Ernie Pyle's typewriter and Columbus's letter to Queen Isabella about discovering the New World; and experience news as it's breaking. The Newseum can be reached by foot from the Key Bridge; it's two blocks from the Rosslyn Metro. ⊠ *1101 Wilson Blvd., Arlington, VA,* ☎ *888/639–7386.* ⊑ *Free.* ⊙ *Wed.–Sun. 10–5. Metro: Rosslyn.*

Pentagon. This is, quite simply, the largest office building in the world. Actually, the Pentagon is not one but five concentric buildings, collectively as wide as three Washington Monuments laid end to end, covering 34 acres. The buildings are connected by 17½ mi of corridors through which 23,000 military and civilian personnel pass each day. There are 691 drinking fountains, 7,754 windows, and a blizzard of other eye-popping statistics. Astonishingly, all this was completed in 1943 after just two years of construction.

The escalator from the Pentagon Metro station surfaces right in the gargantuan office building. The 75-minute tour takes you past only those areas that are meant to be seen by outside visitors. In other words, you won't see situation rooms, communications centers, or gigantic maps outlining U.S. and foreign troop strengths. A uniformed serviceman or -woman (who conducts the entire tour walking backward, lest anyone slip away down a corridor) will take you through hallways lined with the portraits of past and present military leaders, scale models of U.S. Air Force planes and U.S. Navy ships, and the Hall of Heroes, where the names of all the Congressional Medal of Honor winners are inscribed. Occasionally you'll catch a glimpse through an interior window of the Pentagon's 5-acre interior courtyard. A photo ID is required for admission; children under 16 must be accompanied by an adult. ⊠ *Off I–395, Arlington, VA,* ☎ *703/695–1776.* ⊑ *Free.* ⊙ *Tour weekdays every ½ hr 9:30–3:30.*

Ramsay House. The best place to start a tour of Alexandria's Old Town is at the **Alexandria Convention & Visitors Association,** in Ramsay House, the home of the town's first postmaster and lord mayor, William Ramsay. The structure is believed to be the oldest house in Alexandria. Travel counselors here provide brochures and maps for self-guided walking tours. You're given a 24-hour permit that allows you to park free at any two-hour metered spot. ⊠ *221 King St., Alexandria, VA,* ☎ *703/838–4200 or 800/ 388–9119, 703/838–6494 TDD.* ☉ *Daily 9–5.*

Stabler-Leadbeater Apothecary. Once patronized by George Washington and the Lee family, the Stabler-Leadbeater Apothecary is the second-oldest of its kind in the country (the oldest is reputedly in Bethlehem, PA). It was here, on October 17, 1859, that Lt. Col. Robert E. Lee received orders to move to Harper's Ferry to suppress John Brown's insurrection. The shop now houses a small museum of 18th- and 19th-century apothecary memorabilia, including one of the finest collections of apothecary bottles in the country (some 800 bottles in all). ⊠ *105–107 S. Fairfax St., Alexandria, VA,* ☎ *703/836–3713.* ▦ *$2.50.* ☉ *Mon.– Sat. 10–4, Sun. 1–5.*

Tomb of the Unknowns. The first burial at the Tomb of the Unknowns took place at Arlington National Cemetery on November 11, 1921, when the Unknown Soldier from "The Great War" was interred under the large white-marble sarcophagus. Unknown servicemen killed in World War II and Korea were buried in 1958. The unknown serviceman killed in Vietnam was laid to rest on the plaza on Memorial Day 1984. Soldiers from the Army's U.S. 3rd Infantry keep watch over the tomb 24 hours a day, regardless of weather conditions. Each sentinel marches exactly 21 steps, then faces the tomb for 21 seconds, symbolizing the 21-gun salute, America's highest military honor. West of the tomb are memorials to the astronauts killed in the *Challenger* shuttle explosion and to the servicemen killed in 1980 while trying to rescue American hostages in Iran. Rising beyond that is the main mast from the USS *Maine,* the American ship that was sunk in Havana Harbor in 1898, killing 299 men and sparking the Spanish-American War. ⊠ *End of Crook Walk.*

Torpedo Factory Arts Center. A former munitions plant (naval torpedoes were manufactured here during World War I and World War II), now converted into studios and galleries for some 175 professional artists and artisans, the Torpedo Factory Arts Center is one of Alexandria's most popular attractions. You can view the workshops of printmakers, jewelry makers, sculptors, painters, and potters, and most of the art and crafts are for sale at reasonable prices. The Torpedo Factory complex also houses the Alexandria Archaeology Program. ⊠ *105 N. Union St.,* ☎ *703/838–4565.* ⊠ *Free.* ⊙ *Daily 10–5.*

United States Marine Corps War Memorial. Better known simply as the Iwo Jima, this memorial, despite its familiarity, has lost none of its power to stir the emotions. Honoring marines who have given their lives since the corps was formed in 1775, the statue, sculpted by Felix W. de Weldon, is based on Joe Rosenthal's Pulitzer Prize–winning photograph of five marines and a navy corpsman raising a flag atop Mount Suribachi on the Japanese island of Iwo Jima on February 19, 1945. By executive order, a real flag flies 24 hours a day from the 78-ft-high memorial. On Tuesday evenings at 7 from late May to late August there is a Marine Corps sunset parade on the grounds of the memorial. On parade nights a free shuttle bus (☎ 202/433–6060) runs from the Arlington Cemetery visitors' parking lot. A few words of caution: It is dangerous to visit the memorial after dark.

3 Dining

By
Deborah
Papier

Updated
by Thomas
Head

AS THE NATION'S CAPITAL, Washington hosts an international array of visitors and new residents. This infusion of cultures means that DC restaurants are getting better and better. (And sometimes, cheaper and cheaper: More of the top dining rooms now offer reasonably priced fare and fixed-price specials.) Despite the dearth of ethnic neighborhoods and the kinds of restaurant districts found in many cities, you *can* find almost any type of food here, from Burmese to Ethiopian. Even the French-trained chefs who have traditionally set the standard in fine dining are turning to health-conscious new American cuisine, spicy Southwestern recipes, or appetizer-size Spanish *tapas* for inspiration.

In the city's one officially recognized ethnic enclave, Chinatown (centered on G and H streets NW between 6th and 8th), Burmese, Thai, and other Asian cuisines add variety to the many traditional Chinese restaurants. Chinatown has received a shot in the arm since the opening of the new MCI Arena. This has, indeed, made Chinatown and the area around the Gallery Place Metro station the city's hottest area for new restaurant development, with new microbrewery-restaurants such as the District Chop House and Brewery and a new branch of the city Tex-Mex favorite, the Austin Grill. For fine dining, don't overlook restaurants in the city's luxury hotels (☞ Chapter 4). A less expensive way to experience these nationally recognized dining rooms is a weekday lunch.

Note that although most restaurants are accessible by Metro, some are not. Details on Metro stops are provided when this form of public transportation is realistic. For details on price categories, *see* How to Use This Book *in* On the Road with Fodor's at the front of the book.

Adams-Morgan/Woodley Park

Eighteenth Street NW extending south from Columbia Road is wall-to-wall restaurants, with new ones opening so fast it's almost impossible to track them. Although the area has retained some of its Latin American identity, the new eating establishments tend to be Asian, New American, Italian, and Ethiopian. Parking can be impossible on weekends. The nearest Metro stop—Woodley Park/Zoo— is a 10- to 15-minute walk; although it's a safe stroll at night, it may be more convenient to take a cab. Woodley Park has culinary temptations of its own, with a lineup of popular ethnic restaurants right by the Metro.

African

$$ ✕ **Bukom Café.** Sunny African pop music, a palm-frond and *kente*-cloth decor, and a spicy West African menu brighten this narrow two-story dining room. Appetizers include *moi-moi* (black-eyed peas, tomatoes, and corned beef) and *nklakla* (tomato soup with goat). Entrées range from *egussi* (goat with melon seeds) to *kumasi* (chicken in a peanut sauce) to vegetarian dishes such as *jollof* rice and fried plantains. Live music nightly except Monday as well as late hours (until 2 AM Wednesday–Thursday and Sunday, until 3 AM Friday–Saturday) keep this place hopping. ✉ 2442 18th St. NW, ☎ 202/265–4600. AE, D, MC, V. No lunch. Metro: Woodley Park/Zoo.

$–$$ ✕ **Meskerem.** The cuisine of the East African country of
★ Ethiopia abounds in Adams-Morgan, but Meskerem is distinctive for its bright, appealingly decorated dining room and the balcony, where you can eat Ethiopian-style—seated on the floor on leather cushions, with large woven baskets for tables. Entrées are served on a large piece of *injera*, a sourdough flat bread; you eat family style, and you scoop up mouthful-size portions of the hearty dishes with extra bread. Among Meskerem's specialties are stews made with spicy *berbere* chili sauce; *kitfo*, a buttery beef dish served very rare or raw like steak tartare; and a tangy, green-chili vinaigrette potato salad. ✉ 2434 18th St. NW, ☎ 202/462–4100. AE, DC, MC, V. Metro: Woodley Park/Zoo.

Asian

$$–$$$ ✕ **Straits of Malaya.** Just a few blocks off Dupont Circle, Straits of Malaya serves some of the most exotic food in Washington: Malaysian-Singaporean cuisine that borrows from Chinese, Thai, and Indian cooking. Dishes—among them chicken *satay* (on skewers), five-spice rolls, fiery *laksa* (noodle soup), *udang goreng* (shrimp in coconut milk), and *poh pia* (jicama stir-fried with vegetables)—are lovely combinations of sweet and pepper-hot spices. Dining on the

Adams-Morgan/Woodley Park Dining

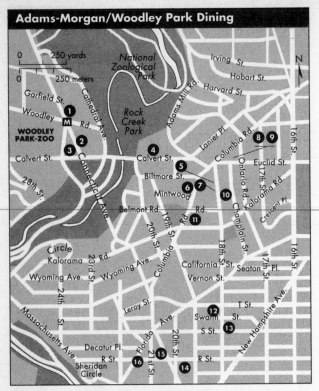

Bukom Café, **5**
Cashion's Eat Place, **6**
City Lights of China, **14**
Grill from Ipanema, **11**
Lauriol Plaza, **13**
Lebanese Taverna, **2**

Mama Ayesha's Restaurant, **4**
Meskerem, **7**
Mixtec, **9**
New Heights, **3**
Nora, **16**
Pasta Mia, **8**
Saigon Gourmet, **1**
Straits of Malaya, **12**

Teaism, **15**
TomTom, **10**

In case you want to see the world.

At American Express, we're here to make your journey a smooth one. So we have over 1,700 travel service locations in over 120 countries ready to help. What else would you expect from the world's largest travel agency?

do more ®

AMERICAN EXPRESS

Travel

http://www.americanexpress.com/travel

In case you want to be welcomed there.

We're here to see that you're always welcomed at establishments everywhere. That's why millions of people carry the American Express® Card – for peace of mind, confidence, and security, around the world or just around the corner.

do more

Cards

In case you're running low.

We're here to help with more than 118,000 Express Cash locations around the world. In order to enroll, just call American Express before you start your vacation.

do more

Express Cash

And just in case.

We're here with American Express® Travelers Cheques and Cheques *for Two*.® They're the safest way to carry money on your vacation and the surest way to get a refund, practically anywhere, anytime.
Another way we help you...

do more

Travelers Cheques

©1997 American Express Travel Related Services Company, Inc.

roof in warm months is one of the city's finer pleasures. ✉ *1836 18th St. NW,* ☎ *202/483–1483. AE, MC, V. No lunch weekends. Metro: Dupont Circle.*

$$ ✕ **Saigon Gourmet.** Service is brisk and friendly at this popular, French-influenced Vietnamese restaurant. The upscale neighborhood patrons return for the ultracrisp *cha-gio* (spring rolls), the savory *pho* (beef broth), seafood soups, and the delicately seasoned and richly sauced entrées. Shrimp Saigon mixes prawns and pork in a peppery marinade, and another Saigon dish—grilled pork with rice crepes—is a Vietnamese variation on Chinese *moo shu.* ✉ *2635 Connecticut Ave. NW,* ☎ *202/265–1360. AE, D, DC, MC, V. Metro: Woodley Park/Zoo.*

$–$$ ✕ **City Lights of China.** The Art-Deco City Lights of China
★ makes the top restaurant critics' lists every year. The traditional Chinese fare is excellent. Less common specialties—among them lamb in a tangy peppery sauce and shark's-fin soup—are deftly cooked as well. Jumbo shrimp are baked in their shells before being stir-fried with ginger and spices. The mint-green booths and elegant silk-flower arrangements conjure up breezy spring days, even in the midst of a frenzied dinner rush. ✉ *1731 Connecticut Ave. NW,* ☎ *202/265–6688. AE, D, DC, MC, V. Metro: Dupont Circle.*

$–$$ ✕ **Teaism.** A novel counterpoint to all the area's coffee bars, Teaism offers not only an impressive selection of more than 50 teas but also delicious Japanese, Indian, and Thai foods. Diners mix small dishes—tandoori kabobs, tea-cured salmon, Indian flat breads, salads, and various chutneys—to create meals or snacks. Japanese *bento* boxes—which contain a salad, entrée, rice, and cookies—are full meals. ✉ *2009 R St. NW,* ☎ *202/667–3827. Reservations not accepted. AE, MC, V. Metro: Dupont Circle.*

Contemporary

$$$– ✕ **Cashion's Eat Place.** The casual atmosphere of Ann
$$$$ Cashion's very personal restaurant, hung with family photos, shouldn't lead you to underestimate the cooking. The restaurant is usually jammed with regulars who come to feast on Cashion's up-to-date, home-style cooking. Roast chicken, a steak entrée, and several seafood dishes are frequent choices. Side dishes such as garlicky mashed potatoes sometimes upstage the main course. Desserts, made by local celebrity pastry chef Ann Amernick, range from the

homey to the sophisticated. ⊠ *1819 Columbia Rd. NW,*
☎ *202/797–1819. MC, V. Closed Mon. No lunch Tues.–*
Sat. Metro: Woodley Park/Zoo.

$$$–   ✕ **New Heights.** This inviting restaurant has large windows
$$$$ that overlook nearby Rock Creek Park. Chef Matthew
Lake's much-acclaimed New American cooking blends the
bold flavors of Asia and the Southwest into the traditional
dishes of the American repertoire. Oysters may be tradi-
tionally fried in a buttermilk batter and then served with
a green chili relish. Sunday brunch is a particular treat in
this lovely room. ⊠ *2317 Calvert St. NW,* ☎ *202/234–4110.*
AE, D, DC, MC, V. No lunch Mon.–Sat. Metro: Woodley
Park/Zoo.

$$$–   ✕ **Nora.** Although it bills itself as an "organic restaurant,"
$$$$ Nora is no collective-run juice bar. The food, like the quilt-
decorated dining room, is sophisticated and attractive. Pep-
pered beef carpaccio with Manchego cheese is a good
starter. Entrées—such as seared rockfish with artichoke
broth and grilled lamb chops with white-bean ragu—ex-
emplify the chef's emphasis on well-balanced, complex ingredients. Warm chocolate cake with cappuccino ice cream
and pear-and-blueberry crisp with praline ice cream are
among the sublime desserts. ⊠ *2132 Florida Ave. NW,* ☎
202/462–5143. MC, V. Closed Sun. No lunch. Metro:
Dupont Circle.

Eclectic

$$–$$$ ✕ **TomTom.** TomTom's trendy menu features pizza baked
in a wood-burning oven and tapas of all sorts—not just traditional Spanish appetizers but also Italian and New American variations. Green salads topped with shrimp or grilled
chicken are fresh and generously portioned. Desserts include
the sinful *boca negra,* a baked chocolate truffle topped
with cinnamon whipped cream. But the real draw is the
atmosphere: On warm nights the rooftop is packed and area
artists set up easels to paint while patrons watch. ⊠ *2333*
18th St. NW, ☎ *202/588–1300. AE, D, DC, MC, V.*
Closed Tues. No lunch. Metro: Woodley Park/Zoo.

Italian

$–$$ ✕ **Pasta Mia.** Pasta Mia's southern Italian appetizers and
entrées all cost a palatable $7–$9. Large bowls of steam-
ing pasta are served with a generous layer of fresh-grated

Parmesan. Best-sellers include fusilli with broccoli and whole cloves of roasted garlic, rich spinach fettuccine verde, and spicy penne *arrabiata*. Served in a teacup the Tiramisu with espresso-soaked ladyfingers is an elegant way to finish a meal. ⊠ *1790 Columbia Rd. NW,* ☎ *202/328–9114. MC, V. Closed Sun. No lunch. Metro: Woodley Park/Zoo.*

Latin American

$$–$$$ ✕ **Grill from Ipanema.** The Grill focuses on Brazilian cuisine, from spicy seafood stews to grilled steak and other hearty meat dishes. Appetizers include fried yucca with spicy sausages and—for adventurous eaters—fried alligator. Second Lady Tipper Gore adores the *mexilhão á carioca*, garlicky mussels cooked in a clay pot. Traditional feijoada is served every day. ⊠ *1858 Columbia Rd. NW,* ☎ *202/986–0757. AE, D, DC, MC, V. No lunch weekdays. Metro: Woodley Park/Zoo.*

$$–$$$ ✕ **Lauriol Plaza.** A charming corner enclave on the border of Adams-Morgan and Dupont Circle, Lauriol Plaza serves Latin American and Spanish dishes—ceviche, paella, and so on—in winning combinations. Such rustic entrées as *lomo saltado* (Peruvian-style strip steak with onions, tomatoes, and fiery jalapeño peppers) are specialties. The simply decorated dining room can get noisy; the alfresco terrace is preferable in good weather. ⊠ *1801 18th St. NW,* ☎ *202/ 387–0035. AE, D, DC, MC, V. Metro: Dupont Circle.*

Mexican

$–$$ ✕ **Mixtec.** At this truly Mexican restaurant, don't expect tortilla chips as a starter—they simply don't serve them. They do, however, offer a trio of delicious salsas to season their array of authentic dishes. Unlike their fast-food counterparts that are topped with lettuce and cheese, the tacos *al carbon* here consist only of grilled beef or pork and fresh corn tortillas; grilled spring onions are a nice accompaniment. Fajitas, enchiladas, and seafood are cooked in the regional styles of Veracruz, Mazatlán, and Acapulco. The *licuados* (fruit drinks) are refreshing complements to the sometimes spicy dishes. ⊠ *1792 Columbia Rd. NW,* ☎ *202/ 332–1011. No reservations. MC, V. Metro: Woodley Park/Zoo.*

Middle Eastern

$$ ✕ **Lebanese Taverna.** Arched ceilings, cedar panels etched with intricate leaf patterns, woven rugs, and brass lighting fixtures give the Taverna a feeling of warm elegance. Be sure to start your meal with an order of Arabic bread that's baked in a wood-burning oven. Small, fried pies filled with spinach, cheese, or meat are buttery and surprisingly light. Lamb, beef, chicken, and seafood are either grilled on kabobs, slow-roasted, or smothered with a garlicky yogurt sauce. A glass of *arak,* a strong, anise-flavored liqueur, makes an excellent digestif. ⊠ *2641 Connecticut Ave. NW,* ☎ *202/265–8681; AE, D, DC, MC, V. Metro: Woodley Park/Zoo.*

$$ ✕ **Mama Ayesha's Restaurant.** Journalists and politicians are known to frequent Ayesha's for the reasonably priced fare. At the family-run eatery, staples such as chicken and lamb kabobs can be had for less than $10, baskets of complimentary pita bread are served hot, and the crisp falafels are some of the best in town. Weekends bring Arabic bands and belly dancing. ⊠ *1967 Calvert St. NW,* ☎ *202/232–5431. AE, DC, MC, V. Metro: Woodley Park/Zoo.*

Capitol Hill

The Hill has a number of bar-eateries that cater to Congressional types in need of fortification after a day spent running the country. Your dining options are augmented by Union Station, which contains some decent—if pricey— restaurants and a large food court offering quick bites that range from barbecue to sushi.

American

$$–$$$$ ✕ **Monocle.** This, the nearest restaurant to the Senate side of the Capitol, is an institution. It's a great place to spot members of Congress at lunch and dinner. The regional American cuisine is rarely adventurous but is thoroughly reliable. The crab cakes, either as a platter or a sandwich, are notable, and specials vary daily. Still, the draw is the old-style Capitol Hill atmosphere. ⊠ *107 D St. NE,* ☎ *202/546–4488. AE, DC, MC, V. Closed weekends. Metro: Union Station.*

French

$$-$$$$ ✕ **La Colline.** Chef Robert Gréault has worked to make La
★ Colline one of the city's best French restaurants. The seasonal menu emphasizes fresh vegetables and seafood, with offerings that range from simple grilled preparations to fricassees and gratins with imaginative sauces. Other choices include duck with orange or cassis sauce and veal with chanterelle mushrooms. ✉ *400 N. Capitol St. NW,* ☎ *202/737–0400. AE, DC, MC, V. Closed Sun. No lunch Sat. Metro: Union Station.*

Seafood

$$-$$$$ ✕ **Phillip's Flagship.** The best of the enormous seafood restaurants that overlook the Capital Yacht Club's marina, Phillip's cavernous rooms and capacious decks are fully capable of accommodating the crowds from the tour buses that fill the parking lot. There's a sushi bar and seafood buffet from Monday to Saturday, a party room with its own deck, and space for 1,400. Despite its size, the restaurant is distinguished by the quality of its raw materials, such as local fish and crab. ✉ *900 Water St. SW,* ☎ *202/488–8515. AE, D, DC, MC, V. Metro: L'Enfant Plaza.*

Southern

$$-$$$ ✕ **B. Smith's.** The DC location of Southern-influenced B. Smith's bears the distinctive mark of chef James Oakley. For appetizers, try the grilled cheddar cheese grits, jambalaya, or seafood croquettes—but skip the overly breaded fried green tomatoes and the too-sweet sweet potatoes. Signature entrée Swamp Thing—a mix of mustard-seasoned shrimp and crawfish with collard greens—is delicious. Desserts are comforting classics, slightly dressed up, like bananas Foster and sweet-potato pecan pie. ✉ *50 Massachusetts Ave. NE (in Union Station),* ☎ *202/289–6188. AE, D, DC, MC, V. Metro: Union Station.*

Downtown

The "new downtown," centered at Connecticut Avenue and K Street, has many of the city's blue chip law firms and deluxe eateries—places that feed off expense-account diners and provide the most elegant atmosphere, most attentive service, and often the best food. But the "old

Washington Dining

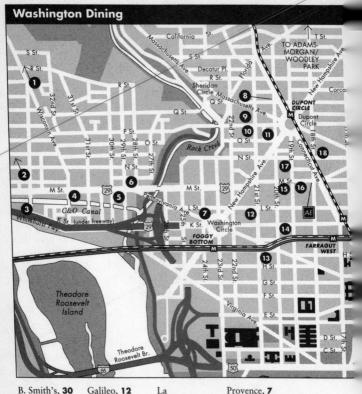

B. Smith's, **30**	Galileo, **12**	La Chaumière, **6**	Provence, **7**
Bistro Français, **4**	Georgia Brown's, **20**	La Colline, **28**	Red Sage, **25**
Bombay Club, **22**	Gerard's Place, **23**	Lespinasse, **21**	Ruppert's, **35**
Burma, **31**	Hibiscus Café, **3**	Li Ho, **32**	Sala Thai, **11**
Café Japone, **10**	i Ricchi, **17**	Marrakesh, **34**	Sam and Harry's, **16**
Citronelle, **5**	Jaleo, **27**	Monocle, **29**	1789, **2**
Coco Loco, **33**	Kinkead's, **13**	Old Ebbitt Grill, **24**	Sholl's Colonial Cafeteria, **14**
Gabriel, **9**		Phillip's Flagship, **26**	

Skewers/Café
Luna, **19**
Sostanza, **8**
Sushi-Ko, **1**
Tabard Inn, **18**
Vidalia, **15**

downtown," farther east, is where the action is these days. Chinatown is booming, and restaurants of all stripes (usually casual and moderately priced) have sprung up to serve the crowds that attend games at the MCI Arena.

African

$$ ★ ✕ **Marrakesh.** A happy surprise is Marrakesh, a bit of Morocco in a part of the city better known for auto-supply shops. The menu is a fixed-price ($24) feast shared by everyone at your table and eaten without silverware (flat bread is used as a scoop). Appetizers consist of a platter of three salads followed by *b'stella*, a chicken version of Morocco's traditional pigeon pie. For the first main course, choose from several chicken preparations. A beef or lamb dish is served next, followed by vegetable couscous, fresh fruit, mint tea, and pastries. Belly dancers put on a nightly show. ⊠ *617 New York Ave. NW, ☎ 202/393–9393. Reservations essential. No credit cards. Lunch only for large groups by reservation. Metro: Gallery Place/Chinatown.*

American

$$$– $$$$ ✕ **Sam and Harry's.** Cigar-friendly Sam and Harry's is understated, genteel, and packed at lunch and dinner. Although the miniature crab cakes are a good way to begin, the real draws are such prime meats as porterhouse and New York strip steaks served on the bone. End the meal with warm pecan pie laced with melted chocolate or a "turtle cake" full of caramel and chocolate that's big enough for two. ⊠ *1200 19th St. NW, ☎ 202/296–4333. AE, D, DC, MC, V. Closed Sun. No lunch Sat. Metro: Dupont Circle.*

$$–$$$ ✕ **Old Ebbitt Grill.** People flock here to drink at the several bars, which seem to go on for miles, and to enjoy carefully prepared bar food that includes buffalo chicken wings, hamburgers, and Reuben sandwiches. The Old Ebbitt also has Washington's most popular oyster bar. Despite the crowds, the restaurant never feels cramped, thanks to its well-spaced, comfortable booths. Service can be slow at lunch; if you're in a hurry try the quick, café-style Ebbitt Express next door. ⊠ *675 15th St. NW, ☎ 202/347–4800. AE, D, DC, MC, V. Metro: Metro Center.*

$ ✕ **Sholl's Colonial Cafeteria.** Here the slogan is "Where good foods are prepared right, served right, and priced right"— and truer words were never spoken. Suited federal work-

ers line up next to pensioners and students to grab a bite
at this DC institution, which is open for breakfast, lunch,
and an early dinner. Favorites include chopped steak, liver
and onions, and baked chicken and fish for less than $5.
Sholl's is famous for its apple, blueberry, peach, and other
fruit pies: All the desserts are scrumptious and cost around
$1. ⊠ 1990 K St. NW, ☎ 202/296–3065. No credit cards.
No dinner Sun. Metro: Farragut West.

Asian

$–$$$ ✕ **Burma.** The fact that Burma (now called Myanmar) the
country is bordered by India, Thailand, and China gives
an indication of the cuisine at Burma, the Chinatown
restaurant. Curry and tamarind share pride of place with
lemon, cilantro, and soy seasonings. Green Tea Leaf and
other salads leave the tongue with a pleasant tingle. Such
entrées as mango pork, tamarind fish, and *kokang* chicken
are equally satisfying. ⊠ 740 6th St. NW, 2nd floor, ☎ 202/
638–1280. AE, D, DC, MC, V. No lunch weekends. Metro:
Gallery Place/Chinatown.

$–$$ ✕ **Li Ho.** Head for unassuming Li Ho if good Chinese food
in satisfying portions is what you seek. Li Ho's specialties—
including duck soup with mustard greens and Singapore
noodles, a rice noodle dish seasoned with curry and bits of
meat—are favorites among the lunchtime crowd. ⊠ 501
H St. NW, ☎ 202/289–2059. MC, V. Metro: Gallery
Place/Chinatown.

Contemporary

$$$$ ✕ **Ruppert's.** Set at the edge of the wasteland that might
eventually be Washington's new convention center is this
very hip spot. Chef John Cochran makes a point of finding the freshest regional ingredients for his menu, which
changes daily. Look for vegetable soups, game birds, the
mushrooms of the season, and such Southern regional del-
icacies as greens and grits. ⊠ 1017 7th St. NW, ☎ 202/
783–0699. AE, MC, V. Closed Sun–Mon. No lunch except Thurs. Metro: Mt. Vernon Sq./UDC.

$$$–   ✕ **Vidalia.** Inspired by the cooking and the ingredients of
$$$$ the South and the Chesapeake Bay region, Chef Jeffrey
Buben's version of New American cuisine revolves around
the best seasonal fruits, vegetables, and seafood he can
find. Don't miss the roasted onion soup with spoon bread,

the shrimp on yellow grits, or the sensational lemon chess pie. ⊠ *1990 M St. NW,* ☎ *202/659–1990. AE, D, DC, MC, V. No lunch Sat–Sun. Metro: Dupont Circle.*

Eclectic

$$$–
$$$$

✕ **Kinkead's.** This multichambered restaurant includes a downstairs pub and raw bar and more formal dining rooms upstairs. The open kitchen upstairs allows you to watch Kinkead and company turn out an eclectic menu of mostly seafood dishes, inspired by chef Robert Kinkead's New England roots and by the cooking of Asia and Latin America. Main-course soups and seafood stews, such as Scandinavian salmon stew, are specialties. The menu also has a selection of simply grilled fish, without sauces. Save room for dessert—the chocolate *dacquoise* (layer cake) is a knockout. ⊠ *2000 Pennsylvania Ave. NW,* ☎ *202/296–7700. AE, DC, MC, V. Metro: Foggy Bottom.*

French

$$$$

✕ **Lespinasse.** The Washington Lespinasse, in the Carlton Hotel, may well be the most beautiful dining room in DC, and although the prices are high, they're justified by the quality of the food and service. Chef Troy Dupuy's menu changes seasonally; courses may include fresh seafood (pan-roasted lobster with napa cabbage is a lovely dish) and lamb three ways—a single plate with a rack, a piece of the loin, and slices of the roast leg. The $36 fixed-price lunch menu is a good way to sample Dupuy's cooking. ⊠ *923 16th St. NW,* ☎ *202/879-6900. AE, D, DC, MC, V. Closed Sun. No lunch Sat. Metro: Farragut North.*

$$$–
$$$$
★

✕ **Gerard's Place.** Don't let the simplicity of the name cause you to underestimate the quality of the cooking at this sophisticated spot owned by acclaimed French chef Gerard Pangaud. In the striking gray and burnt umber dining room, you're served dishes that have intriguing combinations of ingredients. The menu, which changes daily, might include Gerard's signature poached lobster with a ginger, lime, and Sauternes sauce or venison served with dried fruits and pumpkin and beetroot purees. Desserts—such as the chocolate tear, a teardrop-shape flourless chocolate cake veined with raspberry—are exquisite. ⊠ *915 15th St. NW,* ☎ *202/737–4445. AE, DC, MC, V. Closed Sun. No lunch Sat. Metro: McPherson Square*

Indian

$$–$$$ ✕ **Bombay Club.** One block from the White House and a
★ favorite restaurant of the First Family, the beautiful Bom-
bay Club tries to re-create the kind of solace the Beltway
elite might have found in a private club had they been
19th-century British colonials in India rather than late-
20th-century Washingtonians. The bar, which serves hot hors
d'oeuvres at cocktail hour, is furnished with rattan chairs
and paneled with dark wood. The dining room, with pot-
ted palms and a bright blue ceiling above white plaster mold-
ings, is elegant and decorous. The menu includes unusual
seafood specialties and a large number of vegetarian dishes,
but the real standouts are the breads and the seafood appetizers. ⊠ *815 Connecticut Ave. NW,* ☎ *202/659–3727.
AE, DC, MC, V. No lunch Sat. Metro: Farragut West.*

Italian

$$$$ ✕ **Galileo.** The flagship restaurant of Washington entre-
★ preneur-chef Roberto Donna serves sophisticated Pied-
montese-style cooking. The specials vary daily, but to get
the full Galileo experience, order an antipasto, a pasta (perhaps split between two), and a main course of grilled fish,
game, or veal. Preparations are generally simple: The veal
chop might be served with mushroom-and-rosemary sauce,
the beef with black-olive sauce and polenta. The $65 five-
course fixed-price menu is a good value. In a move unusual
for downtown restaurants, Galileo is open for breakfast on
weekdays. ⊠ *1110 21st St. NW,* ☎ *202/293–7191. AE, D,
DC, MC, V. No lunch weekends. Metro: Foggy Bottom.*

$$$– ✕ **i Ricchi.** An airy dining room decorated with terra-cotta
$$$$ tiles, cream-color archways, and floral frescoes, i Ricchi is
★ priced for expense accounts and remains a favorite of crit-
ics and upscale crowds for its earthy Tuscan cuisine. The
spring-summer menu includes such offerings as rolled pork
and rabbit roasted in wine and fresh herbs, and skewered
shrimp; the fall-winter bill of fare brings grilled lamb chops,
thick soups, and sautéed beef fillet. ⊠ *1220 19th St. NW,*
☎ *202/835–0459. AE, DC, MC, V. Closed Sun. No lunch
Sat. Metro: Dupont Circle.*

Latin American

$$–$$$ ✕ **Coco Loco.** People come here for the Mexican tapas,
which are generally washed down with wine or beer. Fa-

vorites include shrimp stuffed with white cheese and wrapped in bacon, duck enchiladas, and *chiles rellenos* (stuffed chiles) in a tomato-cream puree. If you're into serious meat-eating, try the Brazilian-style *churrasqueria*—a parade of skewered grilled meats that are brought to your table and sliced onto your plate. Friday and Saturday nights, half the restaurant becomes an upscale nightclub. ✉ *810 7th St. NW,* ☎ *202/289–2626. AE, MC, V. Closed Sun. No lunch Sat. Metro: Gallery Place/Chinatown.*

Southern

$$–$$$　✕ **Georgia Brown's.** The airy, curving dining room has white honeycomb windows and an unusual ceiling ornamentation of bronze ribbons. An elegant "new South" eatery and a favorite hangout of local politicians, Georgia Brown's serves shrimp Carolina-style (with the head on and steaming grits on the side), beef tenderloin medallions with a bourbon-pecan sauce, and thick, rich crab soup. Fried green tomatoes are given the gourmet treatment, as is the sweet-potato cheesecake. ✉ *950 15th St. NW,* ☎ *202/393–4499. AE, DC, MC, V. No lunch Sat. Metro: McPherson Square*

Southwestern

$$–$$$$　✕ **Red Sage.** This upscale rancher's delight near the White House has a multimillion-dollar decor with a barbed-wire-and-lizard theme and a pseudo-adobe warren of dining rooms. Upstairs are the chile bar and café, where thrifty trendsetters can enjoy a comparatively inexpensive Tex-Mex menu. Downstairs, owner Mark Miller's Berkeley–Santa Fe background surfaces in elaborate, artful presentations of such tony chow as roasted Virginia buffalo with wild shrimp and stuffed game birds with mushroom-jerky salsa. ✉ *605 14th St. NW,* ☎ *202/638–4444. AE, D, DC, MC, V. No lunch Sun. Metro: Metro Center.*

Spanish

$$–$$$　✕ **Jaleo.** This lively Spanish bistro encourages you to make
★　　a meal out of its long list of tapas, although such entrées as grilled fish and paella—which comes in four versions—are just as tasty. Tapas menu highlights are *gambas al ajillo* (sautéed garlic shrimp), fried potatoes with spicy tomato sauce, and *pinchitos* (a skewer of grilled chorizo) with garlic mashed potatoes. For dessert, don't miss the crisp, buttery apple Charlotte and the chocolate hazelnut tart. ✉ *480*

7th St. NW, ☎ *202/628–7949. AE, D, MC, V. Metro: Gallery Place/Chinatown.*

Dupont Circle

South from U Street and north from K Street is Dupont Circle, around which a number of restaurants are clustered. You'll also find a variety of cafés, most with outdoor seating. The District's better gay-friendly establishments are here as well, especially along 17th Street. Chains like Starbuck's and Hannibal's have put fancy coffee on every corner, but long-established espresso bars, like the 24-hour Afterwords (in a bookstore), are a better source for breakfast and light or late fare.

Asian

$$–$$$ ✕ **Café Japone.** The dark interior here has an alternative-scene edge. Most weeknights after 10 PM you're likely to find Japanese businessmen and students, happy from good food and sake, belting out the latest Asian pop songs accompanied by music from a karaoke sound system. On Wednesday and Thursday nights, there's a live jazz band and a mellower crowd. The sushi is nothing to rave about, but it's good, and the kitchen stays open until 1:30 AM during the week, 2:30 AM on weekends. ✉ *2032 P St. NW,* ☎ *202/223–1573. AE, MC, V. No lunch. Metro: Dupont Circle.*

$$–$$$ ✕ **Sala Thai.** Who says Thai food has to be scalp-sweating hot? Sala Thai will make the food as spicy as you wish, but the chef is interested in flavor, not fire. Among the subtly seasoned offerings are *panang goong* (shrimp in curry-peanut sauce), chicken sautéed with ginger and pineapple, and flounder with a choice of four sauces. Mirrored walls and soft lights soften the ambience of this small downstairs dining room with friendly service and a largely neighborhood clientele. ✉ *2016 P St. NW,* ☎ *202/872–1144. AE, DC, MC, V. Metro: Dupont Circle.*

Contemporary

$$$–
$$$$ ✕ **Tabard Inn.** The Hotel Tabard Inn (☞ *also* Chapter 4) meshes an antiques-store sensibility—fading portraits, doilies on overstuffed chairs—with '60s values, serving only organic produce and meat. Appetizers have included

smoked trout cakes with chile-basil mayonnaise; saffron lin-
guine in a tomato-pepper fumet with salmon, oysters, and
monkfish is an example of a colorful main course. The
strongest dishes are such slightly dressed-up classics as the
grilled New York strip steak or the sautéed soft-shell crabs
over wilted greens. Desserts—warm strawberry-rhubarb
crisp or white-chocolate cheesecake—get raves. The courtyard is open in good weather. ⊠ *1739 N St. NW,* ☎ *202/
833-2668. AE, DC, MC, V. Metro: Dupont Circle.*

Italian

$$$ ✕ **Sostanza.** An experimental collaboration between two
established Washington Italian restaurateurs, Sostanza,
which until recently was called Vincenzo, bills itself as an
Italian steak house. The specialty is *bistecca alla fiorentina,*
a Florentine specialty made here with beef from an Italian
breed raised in Virginia rather than the famous Chianina
beef of Italy. The restaurant has few peers in simple seafood
preparations. Part of the dining room is in an airy, glass-
roof courtyard. ⊠ *1606 20th St. NW,* ☎ *202/667-0047.
AE, DC, MC, V. Metro: Dupont Circle.*

Latin American

$$–$$$$ ✕ **Gabriel.** Gabriel takes a nouvelle approach to traditional Latin American and Spanish dishes. *Pupusas,* Sal-
vadoran meat patties, are filled with chorizo and grilled
scallops. The brunch buffet is truly outstanding: In addition to traditional breakfast items, you can enjoy whole suck-
ling pig and made-to-order quesadillas from the carving table,
or Mediterranean specialties like paella, cassoulet, and salads. The dessert table offers tiny fruit tarts, various cheese-
cakes, cookies, and decadent chocolate items. ⊠ *2121 P
St. NW,* ☎ *202/956-6690. AE, D, DC, MC, V. No lunch
weekends. Metro: Dupont Circle.*

Middle Eastern

$–$$ ✕ **Skewers/Café Luna.** As the name implies, the focus at Skew-
ers is on kabobs, here served with almond-flaked rice or pasta.
Lamb with eggplant and chicken with roasted pepper are the
most popular variations, but vegetable kabobs and skewers
of filet mignon and shrimp are equally tasty. If the restaurant is too crowded, you can enjoy the cheap eats (salads,
sandwiches, vegetable lasagna, and pizza) downstairs at

Café Luna. ⊠ *1633 P St. NW,* ☎ *202/387–7400 (Skewers),*
202/387–4005 (Café Luna), or *202/332–2543 (Luna Books).*
AE, DC, MC, V. Metro: Dupont Circle.

Georgetown/West End/Glover Park

In Georgetown, whose central intersection is Wisconsin Avenue and M Street, you'll find white-tablecloth establishments next door to hole-in-the-wall joints. The closest Metro stop is Foggy Bottom, a 15- to 20-minute walk away; consult the Georgetown map before you set out, and consider just taking a cab. Restaurants in the adjacent West End—bounded roughly by Rock Creek Park to the west, N Street to the north, 20th Street to the east, and K Street to the south—are worth checking out as well. Heading north from Georgetown on Wisconsin Avenue, you'll find a cluster of good restaurants in the Glover Park area, including the city's best sushi bar, Sushi-Ko.

Asian

$$–$$$ ✕ **Sushi-Ko.** At the city's best Japanese restaurant, daily spe-
★ cials are always innovative: Sesame-oil seasoned trout is layered with crisp wonton crackers, and a sushi special might be salmon topped with a touch of mango sauce and a tiny spring of dill or thin pieces of scallop with a touch of pesto sauce. And you won't find their whimsical desserts—green-tea ice cream or sake sorbet—at the local Baskin Robbins. ⊠ *2309 Wisconsin Ave. NW,* ☎ *202/333–4187. AE, MC, V. No lunch Sat.–Mon.*

Caribbean

$$–$$$$ ✕ **Hibiscus Café.** African masks and multicolor neon ac-
★ cents hang from the ceiling of this mod restaurant, where weekend crowds are drawn by spicy jerk chicken, blackened fish, shrimp curry, and flavorful soups (try the butternut-ginger bisque). Perfectly fried calamari and a generous piece of shark in a pocket of fried bread are paired with ginger sauce or tangy pineapple chutney to make delectable starters. Desserts—banana mousse with rum sauce, coconut crème brûlée—favor island fruits. ⊠ *3401 K St. NW,* ☎ *202/965–7170. AE, D, MC, V. Closed Mon. No lunch.*

Contemporary

$$$$ ✕ **Citronelle.** California-French chef Michel Richard's flag-
★   ship restaurant, in the Latham Hotel (☞ *also* Chapter 4),
        has his signature glass-front kitchen, which lets you see all
        the action. Richard's appetizer specials might include an im-
        pressive "tart" of thinly sliced grilled scallops that look like
        pale white coins resting on puff pastry. Leek-encrusted
        salmon steak is topped by a crisp fried-potato lattice.
        Desserts are equally luscious: The crunchy napoleon—lay-
        ers of caramelized phyllo dough between creamy vanilla cus-
        tard—is drizzled with butterscotch and dark chocolate. ⊠
        3000 M St. NW, ☎ *202/625–2150. AE, DC, MC, V.*

$$$– ✕ **1789.** The elegant sage-green dining room, with Early
$$$$ American paintings and a fireplace, could easily be a room
★   in the White House. But though the decor is proper and
        genteel, the food is down-to-earth and delicious. Soups, such
        as the rich black bean soup with unsweetened chocolate and
        the seafood stew, are flavorful. Rack of lamb and fillet of
        beef are specialties, and seared tuna stands out among the
        excellent seafood dishes. Service is fluid and attentive.
        Hazelnut chocolate bars with espresso sauce will pep you
        up for a night on the town. ⊠ *1226 36th St. NW,* ☎ *202/
        965–1789. AE, D, DC, MC, V. No lunch.*

French

$$$$ ✕ **Provence.** Lavish simplicity seems to be the key here, from
★   the amber-hued dining room decorated with terra-cotta tiles
        to the fresh herbs that flavor every entrée. Provence's ex-
        tensive menu is enhanced with a daunting list of daily spe-
        cials recited by the server. For appetizers there might be a
        salad of wild greens topped with roasted pigeon and cool
        foie gras. Lobster might be cooked in butter and served with
        a bright red beet sauce or prepared with white truffle oil
        and parsley. The almond cake, served buttery and warm
        with sorbet, ends the meal on a light but decadent note. ⊠
        2401 Pennsylvania Ave. NW, ☎ *202/296–1166. Reserva-
        tions essential. AE, DC, MC, V. Closed Sun. No lunch Sat.
        Metro: Foggy Bottom.*

$$–$$$$ ✕ **Bistro Français.** Washington's chefs head for Bistro
        Français for the minute steak maître d'hôtel or the sirloin
        with black pepper or red wine sauce. Daily specials may
        include *suprême* of salmon with broccoli mousse and beurre
        blanc. The restaurant is divided into two parts—the café

side and the more formal dining room; the café menu includes sandwiches and omelets in addition to entrées. The Bistro also offers $11.95 fixed-price lunches and $17.95 early and late-night dinner specials. It stays open until 3 AM Sunday–Thursday, 4 AM Friday–Saturday. ✉ *3128 M St. NW,* ☎ *202/338–3830. AE, DC, MC, V.*

$$–$$$ ✕ **La Chaumière.** A favorite of Washingtonians seeking an escape from the hurly-burly of Georgetown, La Chaumière (which means "the thatched cottage") has the rustic charm of a French country inn. Fish stew, mussels, and scallops are on the regular menu, and there are always several grilled fish specials. Many local diners plan their meals around La Chaumière's specials, particularly the couscous on Wednesday and the tasty cassoulet on Thursday. ✉ *2813 M St. NW,* ☎ *202/338–1784. AE, DC, MC, V. Closed Sun. No lunch Sat.*

4 Lodging

WITH MORE THAN 340 HOSTELRIES encompassing over 63,000 guest rooms in the DC area, you can always find lodging. Hotels are often full of conventioneers, politicians in transit, or families and school groups in search of museums and monuments. Rates are high around the Cherry Blossom Festival in April. If you're interested in visiting Washington at a calm time—and if you can stand tropical weather—come in August, during the congressional recess. Rates drop in late December and January, except around an inauguration.

By Jan
Ziegler

Updated
by CiCi
Williamson

The properties below were chosen because of their beauty, historical significance, location, or value. All hotels in the $$$ and $$$$ categories have concierges; some in the $$ group do, too (for details on price categories, ☞ How to Use This Book *in* On the Road with Fodor's). Because Washington is an international city, nearly all hotel staffs are multilingual. Hotels' parking fees range from free to $22 a night. This sometimes involves valet parking, with its implied additional gratuities. Street parking is free on Sunday and usually after 6:30 PM. *Read signs carefully*; some are very confusing, and the parking patrol is quick to ticket cars.

To find reasonably priced accommodations in small guest houses and private homes, **Bed 'n' Breakfast Accommodations Ltd. of Washington, D.C.** (⊠ Box 12011, 20005, ☎ 202/328–3510), which is staffed 10–5, is a good source.

Capitol Hill

$$–$$$$ 🏨 **Phoenix Park Hotel.** Named after a historic park in Dublin, the Phoenix Park has an Irish club theme and is home to the Dubliner Pub, where Irish entertainers perform nightly. Across the street from Union Station and only four blocks from the Capitol, this hotel is popular with lobbyists, businesspeople, and tourists. Three penthouse suites have balconies that overlook Union Station; three sophisticated duplex suites have spiral staircases. ⊠ 520 N. Capitol St. NW, 20001, ☎ 202/638–6900 or 800/824–5419, FAX 202/393–3236. 150 rooms, 6 suites. Pub, in-room modem lines,

no-smoking floor, exercise room, laundry service, parking (fee). AE, D, DC, MC, V. Metro: Union Station.

$$–$$$ 🏨 **Holiday Inn on the Hill.** Here you'll find clean, comfortable, low-priced rooms with high-priced views of the Capitol. Both it and Union Station are just two blocks away. Children under age 18 stay free. ⊠ *415 New Jersey Ave. NW, 20001,* ☎ *202/638–1616 or 800/638–1116,* FAX *202/638–0707. 342 rooms. Restaurant, bar, room service, pool, sauna, exercise room, parking (fee). AE, D, DC, MC, V. Metro: Union Station.*

$–$$$ 🏨 **Capitol Hill Suites.** On a quiet residential street behind the Library of Congress, this all-suite hotel's proximity to the House office buildings means that it's often filled with visiting lobbyists when Congress is in session. Guest rooms—which are actually renovated apartments—are large and cozy and have full-size kitchens; the sun-filled lobby has a fireplace. ⊠ *200 C St. SE, 20003,* ☎ *202/543–6000 or 800/ 424–9165,* FAX *202/547–2608. 152 suites. Kitchenettes, parking (fee). AE, DC, V. Metro: Capitol South.*

Downtown

$$$$ 🏨 **Willard Inter-Continental.** Just two blocks from the
★ White House, the Willard—whose present building dates from 1901—has welcomed every American president from Franklin Pierce in 1853 to Dwight Eisenhower in the 1950s, before closing after years of decline. The new Willard, a faithful renovation, is an opulent beaux arts feast for the eye: The main lobby has spectacular proportions, great columns, huge chandeliers, mosaic floors, and elaborately carved ceilings. The hotel's formal eatery, the Willard Room, has won nationwide acclaim. ⊠ *1401 Pennsylvania Ave. NW, 20004,* ☎ *202/628–9100 or 800/327–0200,* FAX *202/637–7326. 340 rooms, 39 suites. 2 restaurants, 2 bars, minibars, room service, health club, laundry service and dry cleaning, meeting rooms, parking (fee). AE, DC, MC, V. Metro: Metro Center.*

$$$– 🏨 **Hay-Adams Hotel.** This Italian Renaissance landmark
$$$$ is located directly across Lafayette Park from the White
★ House. Reserve a room on the south side well in advance to enjoy the city's best view of the mansion and Washington Monument beyond. The Hay-Adams has an eclectic

grandeur inside: European and Asian antiques; Doric, Ionic, and Corinthian touches; carved walnut wainscoting; and intricate ornamental ceilings. It sits on the site of houses owned by statesman and author John Hay and diplomat and historian Henry Adams. The Lafayette dining room serves contemporary American dishes. The hotel's afternoon tea is renowned. ⊠ *1 Lafayette Sq. NW, 20006,* ☎ *202/638–6600 or 800/424–5054,* ℻ *202/638–2716. 125 rooms, 18 suites. Restaurant, bar, room service, laundry service, dry cleaning, parking (fee). AE, DC, MC, V. Metro: Farragut West or Farragut North.*

$$$–
$$$$
★

🏨 **Jefferson Hotel.** Federal-style elegance abounds inside this small luxury hotel. The 100 rooms and suites are each unique in decor and have antiques, original art, VCRs, and CD players; you may borrow from the hotel's video and CD libraries. The Dining Room restaurant is a favorite of high-ranking politicos and film stars. Its American cuisine includes game and seafood. A high staff-to-guest ratio ensures outstanding service: Employees greet you by name, and laundry is hand ironed and delivered in wicker baskets. ⊠ *1200 16th St. NW, 20036,* ☎ *202/347–2200 or 800/368–5966,* ℻ *202/785–1505. 68 rooms, 32 suites. Restaurant, bar, room service, in-room VCRs, laundry service, parking (fee). AE, DC, MC, V. Metro: Farragut North.*

$$$–
$$$$

🏨 **Renaissance Mayflower Hotel.** Franklin Delano Roosevelt wrote "We have nothing to fear but fear itself" in Suite 776, and J. Edgar Hoover ate here at the same table every day for 20 years. Ever since this 10-story hotel opened in 1925 for Calvin Coolidge's inauguration, it has made history makers and leisure travelers feel at home. At this National Historic Landmark, four blocks from the White House, sunlight spills into the majestic skylit lobby, causing the gilded trim to gleam, and Asian rugs splash the floors with color. Contemporary Mediterranean cuisine is served amid silver, crystal, and artful flower arrangements at the Café Promenade restaurant. ⊠ *1127 Connecticut Ave. NW, 20036,* ☎ *202/347–3000 or 800/468–3571,* ℻ *202/466–9082. 660 rooms, 80 suites. 2 restaurants, bar, room service, sauna, exercise room, parking (fee). AE, DC, MC, V. Metro: Farragut North.*

$$$
★

🏨 **Morrison-Clark Inn.** This inn is a merger of two 1864 Victorian town houses that were transformed into the Sol-

Washington Lodging

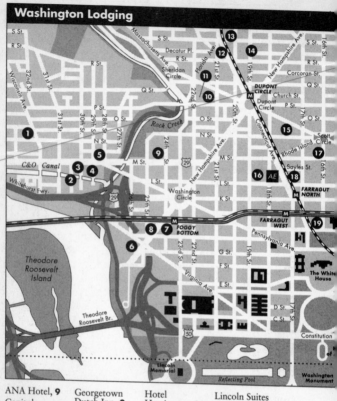

ANA Hotel, **9**

Capitol
Hill Suites, **28**

Channel Inn, **27**

Doubletree
Guest Suites, **7**

Four Seasons
Hotel, **5**

George
Washington
University
Inn, **8**

Georgetown
Dutch Inn, **2**

Georgetown
Inn, **1**

Georgetown
Suites, **4**

Hay-Adams
Hotel, **19**

Henley Park
Hotel, **22**

Holiday Inn on
the Hill, **29**

Hotel
Harrington, **25**

Hotel Sofitel
Washington, **12**

Hotel Tabard
Inn, **15**

Hotel
Washington, **23**

Jefferson
Hotel, **17**

Latham
Hotel, **3**

Lincoln Suites
Downtown, **16**

Loews L'Enfant
Plaza, **26**

Morrison-
Clark Inn, **20**

Normandy
Inn, **14**

Phoenix Park
Hotel, **30**

Radisson Barceló
Hotel, **11**

Renaissance
Mayflower
Hotel, **18**

The Sheraton
Luxury
Collection
Washington,
DC, **10**

Washington
Hilton and
Towers, **13**

Washington
International
AYH-Hostel, **21**

Watergate
Hotel, **6**

Willard Inter-
Continental, **24**

diers, Sailors, Marines and Airmen's Club in 1923. The club served as a military establishment for 57 years; first ladies Mamie Eisenhower and Jacqueline Kennedy volunteered regularly here. One house has a 1917 Chinese Chippendale porch; the antiques-filled public rooms have marble fireplaces, bay windows, 14-foot pier mirrors, and porch access. Rooms have neoclassic, French country, or Victorian furnishings. The inn's highly rated restaurant serves American cuisine with Southern and other regional influences. ⊠ *Massachusetts Ave. and 11th St. NW, 20001,* ☎ *202/898–1200 or 800/332–7898,* FAX *202/289–8576. 54 rooms. CP. Restaurant, minibars, room service, exercise room, laundry service and dry cleaning, parking (fee). AE, D, DC, MC, V. Metro: Mount Vernon Square.*

$$–$$$
★
🏨 **Hotel Washington.** Since opening in 1918, the Hotel Washington has been known for its view. Washingtonians bring visitors to the outdoor rooftop bar—open May to October—for cocktails and a panorama that includes the White House grounds and the Washington Monument. Now a National Landmark, the hotel sprang from the drawing boards of John Carrère and Thomas Hastings, who designed the New York Public Library. Elvis Presley stayed in Suite 506. Color schemes vary from one room to the next, but all rooms have mahogany furniture. ⊠ *515 15th St. NW, 20004,* ☎ *202/638–5900,* FAX *202/638–1594. 344 rooms, 16 suites. 2 restaurants, bar, deli, lobby lounge, room service, exercise room, laundry service and dry cleaning, business services, parking (fee). AE, DC, MC, V. Metro: Metro Center.*

$–$$$
★
🏨 **Henley Park Hotel.** A Tudor-style building adorned with 119 gargoyles, this National Historic Trust hotel has the cozy charm of an English country house. The main eatery, Coeur de Lion, has a leafy atrium, stained-glass windows, and an American menu. Complimentary amenities include hors d'oeuvres and jazz nightly in Marley's Lounge, weekday limousine service to any downtown destination from 7:30 to 9:30 AM, and 24-hour room service. The hotel is an eight-block walk to the Smithsonian museums and a five-block walk to the MCI Sports Arena. ⊠ *926 Massachusetts Ave. NW, 20001,* ☎ *202/638–5200 or 800/222–8474,* FAX *202/638–6740. 79 rooms, 17 suites. Restaurant, bar, in-room modem lines, room service, parking (fee). AE, DC, MC, V. Metro: Metro Center or Gallery Place/Chinatown.*

$–$$ ⊞ **Lincoln Suites Downtown.** The Lincoln Suites (formerly Hotel Anthony) has a small lobby, reasonable prices, and very large guest suites. The center-city hotel's all-suite rooms include either a kitchen or wet bar, refrigerator, and microwave. The friendly staff offers free, freshly baked cookies—served with milk, of course—every evening. Other amenities include free passes to Bally's Health and Fitness Club, free weekend breakfast, and free copies of the *Washington Post* on weekdays. ⊠ *1823 L St. NW, 20036,* ☎ *202/223–4320 or 800/424–2970,* ℻ *202/223–8546. 99 suites. Restaurant, room service. AE, DC, MC, V. Metro: Farragut North.*

$ ⊞ **Hotel Harrington.** Just three blocks from the J. W. Marriott and Grand Hyatt, the Harrington is miles away in price. This is one of Washington's oldest hotels, without frills but with low prices and a location right in the center of everything. It's very popular with springtime high school bus tours and with families, who like the two-bedroom, two-bathroom suites. ⊠ *436 11th St. NW, 20004,* ☎ *202/628–8140 or 800/424–8532,* ℻ *202/347–3924. 236 rooms, 24 suites. Restaurant, cafeteria, pub, room service, barbershop, coin laundry, meeting rooms, parking (fee). AE, D, DC, MC, V. Metro: Metro Center.*

$ ⊞ **Washington International AYH-Hostel.** This well-kept place has bunk beds and a kitchen, laundry room, and living room. Single men and women are in separate rooms; families are given their own room if the hostel is not full. The maximum stay is 29 days. College-age travelers predominate, and July–September is the busiest period. ⊠ *1009 11th St. NW, 20001,* ☎ *202/737–2333,* ℻ *202/737–1508. 250 beds. Kitchen, shop, coin laundry. MC, V. Metro: Metro Center.*

Dupont Circle

$$$$ ⊞ **The Sheraton Luxury Collection Washington, DC.** The childhood home of Al Gore (his father, while a senator, had a residence here), this intimate hotel that was a Ritz-Carlton until August 1997 has an English hunt-club theme with complimentary butler service. The rooms have views of Embassy Row or Georgetown and the National Cathedral. The renowned Jockey Club restaurant, with its half-timber ceilings, dark wood paneling, and red-check table-cloths, draws the crowned heads of Washington. The Fairfax Bar is a cozy spot for a drink beside the fire (with piano entertainment some evenings). ⊠ *2100 Massachusetts Ave. NW, 20008,* ☎ *202/293–2100 or 800/325–3589,* FAX *202/293–0641. 154 rooms, 59 suites. Restaurant, bar, minibars, room service, in-room VCRs, massage, sauna, exercise room, meeting room, parking (fee). AE, DC, MC, V. Metro: Dupont Circle.*

$$$$ 🏨 **Washington Hilton and Towers.** A busy convention hotel
   ★   with extensive meeting and banqueting rooms, the Hilton has guest rooms that are compact and sterile but light-filled, and because the hotel is on a hill, each has a view of the Washington skyline. Shops and restaurants of Dupont Circle and the Adams-Morgan neighborhood are just a short walk away. There are extensive indoor and outdoor athletic facilities. ⊠ *1919 Connecticut Ave. NW, 20009,* ☎ *202/483–3000 or 800/445–8667,* FAX *202/265–8221. 1,062 rooms, 88 suites. 2 restaurants, 2 bars, outdoor café, in-room modem lines, room service, pool, wading pool, sauna, steam room, 3 tennis courts, health club, jogging, shuffleboard, parking (fee). AE, DC, MC, V. Metro: Dupont Circle.*

$$–$$$$ 🏨 **Hotel Sofitel Washington.** Directly across Connecticut
   ★   Avenue from the Hilton, this French-owned hotel has rooms with small work areas. The Trocadero Café serves three meals daily. ⊠ *1914 Connecticut Ave. NW, 20009,* ☎ *202/797–2000 or 800/424–2464,* FAX *202/462–0944. 107 rooms, 37 suites. Restaurant, bar, room service, minibars, exercise room, laundry service and dry cleaning, parking (fee). AE, DC, MC, V. Metro: Dupont Circle.*

$$–$$$ 🏨 **Radisson Barceló Hotel.** Convenient to Dupont Circle and Georgetown, the Barceló was once an apartment building and has large rooms that are especially good for families. The second-floor outdoor swimming pool has a lovely setting—a brick courtyard is enclosed by the walls of the hotel and the backs of a row of century-old town houses to the east. Spanish fare is served at the Gabriel Restaurant. ⊠ *2121 P St. NW, 20037,* ☎ *202/293–3100,* FAX *202/ 857–0134. 235 rooms, 65 suites. Restaurant, bar, tapas bar, room service, sauna, exercise room, parking (fee). AE, D, DC, MC, V. Metro: Dupont Circle.*

$–$$$ 🏨 **Hotel Tabard Inn.** Formed by a linkage of three Victorian town houses, the Hotel Tabard Inn is one of the oldest continuously running hostelries in DC. Named after the inn in Chaucer's *Canterbury Tales*, it's furnished throughout with well-broken-in Victorian and American Empire antiques; the floors are creaky, and the plumbing is old-fashioned. Dim lighting and a genteel shabbiness are off-putting to some and charming to others. The street is quiet, and Dupont Circle and the K Street business district are nearby. Passes are provided to the nearby YMCA, which has extensive fitness facilities. The Tabard's restaurant is popular with locals. ⊠ *1739 N St. NW, 20036,* ☎ *202/785–1277,* ℻ *202/785–6173. 40 rooms, 25 with bath. CP. Restaurant, lobby lounge. MC, V. Metro: Dupont Circle.*

Georgetown

$$$$ 🏨 **Four Seasons Hotel.** The Four Seasons Hotel may be a
★   modern brick-and-glass edifice amid Georgetown's 19th-century Federal and Georgian row houses, but inside Old World elegance prevails. Rich mahogany paneling, antiques, spectacular flower arrangements, and impeccable service are hallmarks of this mecca for Washington's elite. Rooms are spacious and bright and have an incredible array of amenities; some bathrooms have sunken tubs. Views are of the C&O Canal, Rock Creek Park, the busy Georgetown street scene, or the quiet courtyard. Brunch is a treat at this hotel. ⊠ *2800 Pennsylvania Ave. NW, 20007,* ☎ *202/342–0444 or 800/332–3442,* ℻ *202/342–1673. 167 rooms, 70 suites. 2 restaurants, bar, room service, pool, health club, nightclub, concierge, parking (fee). AE, DC, MC, V. Metro: Foggy Bottom.*

$$$$ 🏨 **Georgetown Inn.** With an atmosphere reminiscent of an old gentleman's sporting club, this quiet, European-style, redbrick hotel has an 18th-century flavor. Guest rooms are large and have a colonial-style decor. The hotel is in the heart of historic Georgetown near shopping, dining, galleries and theaters. ⊠ *1310 Wisconsin Ave. NW, 20007,* ☎ *202/333–8900 or 800/424–2979,* ℻ *202/625–1744. 86 rooms, 10 suites. Restaurant, bar, in-room modem lines, room service, exercise room, parking (fee). AE, DC, MC, V. Metro: Foggy Bottom.*

$$$–
$$$$ ☒ **Latham Hotel.** This small Federal-style hotel on George-
town's fashionable main avenue has immaculate, beauti-
fully decorated rooms, many with treetop views of "George's
town," the Potomac River, and the C&O Canal. The hotel
is a favorite of Europeans, world leaders, and celebrities.
The polished brass and glass lobby leads to Citronelle (☞
Chapter 3), which is one of the city's best restaurants; a La
Madeleine bakery/eatery is also on site. Three blocks away
is Georgetown Park, a handsome, upscale shopping mall.
☒ *3000 M St. NW, 20007,* ☏ *202/726–5000 or 800/
368–5922,* FAX *202/337–4250. 143 rooms, 21 suites. 2
restaurants, bar, in-room modem lines, minibars, room
service, pool, parking (fee). AE, DC, MC, V. Metro: Foggy
Bottom.*

$$$ ☒ **Georgetown Dutch Inn.** A half block off M Street,
Georgetown's main thoroughfare, this modest, Georgian-
style all-suite hotel has large guest rooms and kitchens, and
sofa beds and dinette sets in the living rooms. Breakfast
is served in the small lobby decorated with 18th-century
touches. ☒ *1075 Thomas Jefferson St. NW, 20007,* ☏ *202/
337–0900 or 800/388–2410,* FAX *202/333–6526. 47 suites.
CP. Kitchenettes, room service. AE, DC, MC, V. Metro:
Foggy Bottom.*

$$–$$$ ☒ **Georgetown Suites.** If you consider standard hotel rooms
cramped and overpriced, the Georgetown Suites—in a
brick courtyard one block south of M Street in the heart
of Georgetown—is a find. Suites vary in size but all have
large kitchens, irons and ironing boards, hair dryers, and
voice mail. Children under 12 stay free. ☒ *1111 30th St.
NW, 20007,* ☏ *202/298–7800 or 800/348–7203,* FAX *202/
333–5792. 216 suites. CP. Kitchenettes, in-room modem
lines, exercise room, laundry service and dry cleaning,
parking (fee). AE, DC, MC, V. Metro: Foggy Bottom.*

Southwest

$$–$$$$ ☒ **Loews L'Enfant Plaza.** Just two blocks from Smithsonian
museums and atop a shopping mall–office complex and
Metro stop, this hotel was named for the architect who de-
signed Washington. Guest rooms, which are on the top four
floors, have spectacular river, Capitol, or monument views.
The hotel's proximity to several government agencies

(USDA, USPS, USIA, and DOT) makes it popular with business travelers. All rooms have coffeemakers and TVs and phones in both bathrooms and bedrooms. "Club" guest rooms all have fax machines. The American Grill restaurant serves—surprise—regional American food. ✉ *L'Enfant Plaza SW, 20024,* ☎ *202/484–1000 or 800/ 223–0888,* 🖷 *202/646–4456. 348 rooms, 22 suites. Restaurant, 2 bars, minibars, room service, in-room VCRs, indoor pool, health club, parking (fee). AE, DC, MC, V. Metro: L'Enfant Plaza.*

$–$$ 🏨 **Channel Inn.** The only hotel on Washington's waterfront, this property overlooks Washington Channel, the marina, and the Potomac River. The hotel is home to the Pier 7 Restaurant and Engine Room Lounge. Public areas and meetings rooms have a nautical motif with mahogany panels and marine artifacts. The terrace allows scenic cocktail-quaffing and dining in warm weather. The Mall, Smithsonian, Treasury, and several other government offices are close. Access to a nearby health club is free of charge. ✉ *650 Water St. SW, 20024,* ☎ *202/554–2400 or 800/368–5668,* 🖷 *202/863–1164. 100 rooms. Restaurant, bar, outdoor café, pool, meeting rooms, free parking. AE, D, DC, MC, V. Metro: Waterfront.*

Northwest/Upper Connecticut Avenue

$–$$ 🏨 **Normandy Inn.** A small, quaint European-style hotel on
★ a quiet street in the embassy area of Connecticut Avenue, the Normandy is near fine dining and shopping. Rooms are neat, cozy, and attractively decorated; all have refrigerators and coffeemakers. You can select a book from the inn's library and read by the fireplace in the lobby while enjoying the complimentary coffee and tea available in the morning and afternoon. ✉ *2118 Wyoming Ave. NW, 20008,* ☎ *202/ 483–1350 or 800/424–3729,* 🖷 *202/387–8241. 75 rooms. CP. Refrigerators, parking (fee). AE, D, MC, V. Metro: Dupont Circle.*

West End/Foggy Bottom

$$$$ 🏨 **Watergate Hotel.** The Watergate is accustomed to serv-
★ ing the world's elite. The lobby sets a genteel tone with its

classic columns, Asian rugs on black and white checkerboard marble, subdued lighting, and soothing classical music. The hotel is on the Potomac River, across the street from the Kennedy Center, and a short walk from the State Department and Georgetown. Originally intended as apartments, the guest rooms are large, and all have walk-in closets, fax machines, kitchens or wet bars, and refrigerators. The riverside restaurant, Aquarelle, serves sophisticated Euro-American cuisine. There's complimentary limousine service weekdays 7 AM to 10 AM. ⊠ *2650 Virginia Ave. NW, 20037,* ☎ *202/965–2300 or 800/424–2736,* FAX *202/337–7915. 90 rooms, 141 suites. Restaurant, 2 bars, refrigerators, room service, indoor pool, health club, parking (fee). AE, DC, MC, V. Metro: Foggy Bottom.*

$$$–
$$$$
★

🏨 **ANA Hotel.** This Japanese-owned hotel is a stylish combination of the contemporary and the traditional. The beautiful glassed lobby and about a third of the bright, airy rooms have views of the central courtyard and gardens, which are popular for weddings. The hotel's informal restaurant, the Bistro, has the flavor of 19th-century Paris and contains an antique mahogany bar. ⊠ *2401 M St. NW, 20037,* ☎ *202/429–2400 or 800/228–3000,* FAX *202/ 457–5010. 406 rooms, 9 suites. 2 restaurants, bar, café, room service, indoor lap pool, pool, beauty salon, sauna, steam room, health club, parking (fee). AE, DC, MC, V. Metro: Foggy Bottom.*

$$–$$$

🏨 **Doubletree Guest Suites.** In a quiet section of New Hampshire Avenue, close to Kennedy Center, the all-suite Doubletree has a small, European-style lobby, but its suites are large and have full kitchens, separate bedrooms, and living-dining areas with desks, large dining tables, and sofa beds. In-room amenities include irons, ironing boards, and hair dryers. There's an outdoor rooftop pool (a great spot for viewing the DC skyline and Georgetown). Next door to the hotel is Donatello's, an Italian eatery; you can have food from here delivered (and charged) to your room. ⊠ *801 New Hampshire Ave. NW, 20037,* ☎ *202/785–2000 or 800/424–2900,* FAX *202/785–9485. 101 suites. In-room modem lines, kitchenettes, room service, pool, coin laundry, dry cleaning, parking (fee). AE, D, DC, MC, V. Metro: Foggy Bottom.*

$-$$ ▦ **George Washington University Inn.** This reasonably priced gem is in the Foggy Bottom historic area of quiet residential streets a few blocks from Kennedy Center and the State Department. The hostelry is also two blocks from George Washington University, and you have complimentary use of the university's fitness center. The front entrance is through gray wrought iron gates into a courtyard. Beveled glass doors open into a small lobby floored in gray marble. Rooms have Williamsburg-style furniture, hair dryers, irons, ironing boards, refrigerators, microwaves, and coffeemakers. Turndown service, daily newspapers, and shoe shines are complimentary. Zuki Moon, a Japanese noodle house and tea garden, is off the lobby. ⊠ *824 New Hampshire Ave. NW, 20037,* ☎ *202/337–6620 or 800/426–4455,* ℻ *202/298–7499. 48 rooms, 31 suites, 16 efficiencies. Restaurant, in-room modem lines, no-smoking rooms, refrigerators, laundry service, meeting rooms, parking (fee). AE, D, DC, MC, V. Metro: Foggy Bottom.*

5 Nightlife and the Arts

BONUS MILES MAKE
GREAT SOUVENIRS.

Earn Miles With Your MCI Card.

Take the MCI Card along on this trip and start earning miles for the next one. You'll earn frequent flyer miles on all your calls and save with the low rates you've come to expect from MCI. Before you know it, you'll be on your way to some other international destination.

Sign up for MCI by calling
1-800-FLY-FREE

*U.S. dollar equivalent, net of taxes, credits and discounts. All airline program rules and conditions apply. Other terms and conditions apply to ongoing mileage offer and bonus mile offer. MCI, its logo and the names of the products and services referred to herein are proprietary marks of MCI Communications Corporation. American Airlines reserves the right to change the AAdvantage program at any time without notice. American Airlines is not responsible for products and services offered by other participating companies. American Airlines and AAdvantage are registered trademarks of American Airlines, Inc.

Is this a great time, or what? :-)

Earn Frequent Flyer Miles.

AmericanAirlines
A'Advantage

Continental Airlines
OnePass

▲ Delta Air Lines
SkyMiles

HAWAIIAN
AIRLINES

MIDWEST EXPRESS AIRLINES

NORTHWEST AIRLINES
WORLDPERKS

Rapid Rewards
SOUTHWEST AIRLINES

✈ MILEAGE PLUS
United Airlines

US AIRWAYS
DIVIDEND MILES

With guidebooks for every kind of travel—from weekend getaways to island hopping to adventures abroad—it's easy to understand why smart travelers go with **Fodor's**.

At bookstores everywhere.
www.fodors.com

Smart travelers go with **Fodor's**™

THE ARTS

By John F. Kelly

Updated by Holly Bass

In the past 20 years, DC has gone from being a cultural desert to a thriving arts center—a place where national artists develop new works. The Kennedy Center is a world-class venue, home of the National Symphony Orchestra (NSO), now conducted by Leonard Slatkin, and host to Broadway shows, ballet, modern dance, opera, and more. Lines wrap around the block at the National Theatre for such big hit musicals as *Chicago* and *Rent*. Washington even has its own "off-Broadway": A half dozen or so plucky theaters scattered around the city offer new works and new twists on old works. Several art galleries present highly regarded chamber music series.

Several publications have calendars of entertainment events. The *Washington Post* "Weekend" section comes out on Friday, and its "Guide to the Lively Arts" is printed daily. On Thursday, look for the *Washington Times* "Weekend" section and the free weekly *Washington CityPaper*. You might also consult the "City Lights" section in the monthly *Washingtonian* magazine.

Tickets

ProTix (☎ 703/218–6500) takes reservations for events at Arena Stage, Center Stage, Ford's Theatre, the Holocaust Museum, the 9:30 Club, and Signature Theater. It also has outlets in selected Waxie Maxies.

Ticketmaster (☎ 202/432–7328 or 800/551–7328) takes phone charges for events at most venues around the city. You can purchase Ticketmaster tickets in person at all Hecht's department stores. No refunds or exchanges are allowed.

TicketPlace sells half-price, day-of-performance tickets for selected shows; a "menu board" lists available performances. Only cash is accepted, and there's a 10% service charge per order. TicketPlace is also a full-price Ticketmaster outlet. ⊠ *Old Post Office Pavilion, 1100 Pennsylvania Ave. NW, ☎ 202/842–5387. Metro: Federal Triangle. ☉ Tues.– Sat. 11–6. Tickets for Sun. and Mon. performances sold on Sat.*

Concert Halls

DAR Constitution Hall. The 3,700-seat Constitution Hall hosts visiting musicians who perform everything from jazz to pop to rap. ⊠ *18th and C Sts. NW,* ☎ *202/628–4780.*

John F. Kennedy Center for the Performing Arts. Any search for cultured entertainment should start here. The "KenCen" is actually five stages under one roof: the **Concert Hall,** home of the National Symphony Orchestra (NSO); the 2,200-seat **Opera House,** the setting for ballet, modern dance, opera, and large-scale musicals; the **Eisenhower Theater,** usually used for drama; the **Terrace Theater,** a Philip Johnson–designed space that showcases chamber groups and experimental works; and the **Theater Lab,** home to cabaret-style performances (since 1987 the audience-participation hit mystery *Shear Madness* has been playing here). ⊠ *New Hampshire Ave. and Rock Creek Pkwy. NW,* ☎ *202/467–4600 or 800/444–1324.*

Lisner Auditorium. A 1,500-seat theater on the campus of George Washington University, Lisner Auditorium is the setting for pop, classical, and choral music shows as well as modern dance performances and musical theater. ⊠ *21st and H Sts. NW,* ☎ *202/994–6800.*

MCI Arena. This brand-new, 19,000-seat arena is now the home of the Washington Capitals hockey and Washington Wizards basketball teams. It also hosts many concerts, ice-skating events, and the circus. ⊠ *601 F St. NW,* ☎ *202/ 628–3200.*

National Gallery of Art. Free concerts by the National Gallery Orchestra, conducted by George Manos, and performances by visiting recitalists and ensembles are held in the venerable West Building's West Garden Court on Sunday evenings from October to June. Most performances highlight classical music, though April's American Music Festival often features jazz. Entry is first-come, first-served. ⊠ *6th St. and Constitution Ave. NW,* ☎ *202/842–6941 or 202/842–6698.*

Smithsonian Institution. The Smithsonian presents a rich assortment of music—both free and ticketed. Jazz, musical theater, and popular standards are performed in the National Museum of American History. In the third-floor

Hall of Musical Instruments, musicians periodically play historic instruments from the museum's collection. In warm weather shows are held in the courtyard between the National Portrait Gallery and the National Museum of American Art. The **Smithsonian Associates Program** (☎ 202/357–3030) offers everything from a cappella groups to Cajun zydeco bands; many perform in the National Museum of Natural History's Baird Auditorium. ⊠ *Smithsonian Castle: 1000 Jefferson Dr. SW. Baird Auditorium: 10th St. and Constitution Ave. NW,* ☎ *202/357–2700.*

USAirways Arena. The area's top venue for big-name pop, rock, and rap acts seats 20,000. It was formerly the home of the Capitals and Wizards, which now play at the MCI Center (☞ *above*). ⊠ *1 Harry S. Truman Dr., Landover, MD,* ☎ *301/350–3400 or 202/432–7328.*

Dance

Dance Place. A studio theater that presented its first performance in 1980, Dance Place is the site of modern and ethnic dance shows most weekends. ⊠ *3225 8th St. NE,* ☎ *202/269–1600.*

Washington Ballet. Between September and May this company presents classical and contemporary ballets—including works by such choreographers as George Balanchine, Marius Petipa, and Choo-San Goh—at the Kennedy Center (☞ Concert Halls, *above*) and the Warner Theatre (☞ Theater and Performance Art, *below*). Each December the Washington Ballet performs *The Nutcracker.* ☎ *202/362–3606.*

Film

American Film Institute. More than 700 movies—including contemporary and classic foreign and American films—are shown each year at the American Film Institute's theater in the Kennedy Center. Filmmakers and actors are often present to discuss their work. ⊠ *Kennedy Center, New Hampshire Ave. and Rock Creek Pkwy. NW,* ☎ *202/785–4600.*

Filmfest DC. An annual citywide festival of international cinema, the DC International Film Festival, or Filmfest, as it is affectionately known, takes place in late April and early May. Films are shown at various venues throughout the city. You can purchase tickets in advance over the phone; otherwise, ticket sales and seating are on a first-come, first-served basis—and some films *do* sell out. ⊠ *Box 21396, 20009,* ☎ *202/724–5613.*

Hirshhorn Museum. If you love avant-garde and experimental film, check out the weekly movies—often first-run documentaries, features, and short films—that are shown here free. ⊠ *8th and Independence Ave. SW,* ☎ *202/357–2700.*

National Archives. Historical films are shown here daily. ⊠ *8th and Constitution Aves. NW,* ☎ *202/501–5000.*

National Gallery of Art East Building. Free classic and international films (they often complement exhibits) are shown in this museum's large auditorium. ⊠ *4th and Constitution NW,* ☎ *202/737–4215.*

National Geographic Society. Free educational films with a scientific, geographic, or anthropological focus are shown here weekly. ⊠ *17th and M Sts. NW,* ☎ *202/857–7588.*

Music

Chamber Music

Corcoran Gallery of Art. Hungary's Takacs String Quartet and the Cleveland Quartet are among the chamber groups that appear in the Corcoran's Musical Evening Series, one Friday each month from October to May (there are also some summer offerings). ⊠ *17th St. and New York Ave. NW,* ☎ *202/639–1700.*

Folger Shakespeare Library. The library's internationally acclaimed resident chamber music ensemble, the Folger Consort, regularly presents instrumental and vocal pieces from the medieval, Renaissance, and Baroque periods. The season runs from October to May. ⊠ *201 E. Capitol St. SE,* ☎ *202/544–7077.*

National Academy of Sciences. Free performances are given October through May in the academy's 670-seat auditorium, which has almost perfect acoustics. Both the National

Musical Arts Chamber Ensemble and the United States
Marines Chamber Orchestra perform regularly. ⊠ *2101
Constitution Ave. NW,* ☎ *202/334–2436.*

Phillips Collection. Duncan Phillips's mansion is more than
an art museum. From September through May the long,
paneled music room hosts Sunday-afternoon recitals. Chamber groups from around the world perform. ⊠ *1600 21st
St. NW,* ☎ *202/387–2151.*

Choral Music

**Basilica of the National Shrine of the Immaculate Concep-
tion.** Choral and church groups frequently perform in this
impressive venue. ⊠ *Michigan Ave. and 4th St. NE,* ☎ *202/
526–8300.*

Choral Arts Society of Washington. The 180-voice Choral
Arts Society choir performs a varied selection of classical
pieces at the Kennedy Center (☞ Concert Halls, *above*) from
September to June. ☎ *202/244–3669.*

Washington National Cathedral. Choral and church groups
frequently perform in this grand cathedral. Admission to
these events is generally free. ⊠ *Wisconsin and Massachusetts Aves. NW,* ☎ *202/537–6200.*

Opera

Mount Vernon College. The college's intimate Hand Chapel
is the setting for otherwise rarely produced chamber operas each winter and spring. ⊠ *2100 Foxhall Rd. NW,* ☎
202/625–4655.

Washington Opera. Eight operas—presented in their original languages with English supertitles—are performed each
season (November–March) in the Kennedy Center's Opera
House and Eisenhower Theater (☞ Concert Halls, *above*).
Performances are often sold out to subscribers, but you can
purchase returned tickets an hour before curtain time. Stand-
ing-room tickets go on sale at the Kennedy Center box office each Saturday at 10 AM for the following week's
performances. ☎ *202/295–2400 or 800/876–7372.*

Orchestra

National Symphony Orchestra. The season at the Kennedy
Center is from September to June. In summer the NSO per-

forms at Wolf Trap Farm Park (✉ 1551 Trap Rd., ☎ 703/ 255–1900) in Vienna, Virginia, as well as giving free concerts at the Carter Barron Amphitheatre (☞ Performance Series, *below*). ☎ *202/416–8100.*

Performance Series

Carter Barron Amphitheatre. On Saturday and Sunday nights from mid-June to August this lovely, 4,250-seat outdoor theater in Rock Creek Park hosts pop, jazz, gospel, and rhythm-and-blues artists such as Chick Corea, Nancy Wilson, and Tito Puente. ✉ *16th St. and Colorado Ave. NW,* ☎ *202/426–6837 or 202/426–0486 (off-season).*

District Curators. This independent, nonprofit organization presents adventurous contemporary performers from around the world in spaces around the city, mostly in summer (June–August). Much of the group's season is encompassed by its Jazz Arts Festival. Past artists have included Laurie Anderson, Philip Glass, the World Saxophone Quartet, and Cassandra Wilson. ☎ *202/783–0360.*

Ft. Dupont Summer Theater. The National Park Service presents national and international jazz artists at 8:30 on Friday and Saturday evenings from July to August at the outdoor Ft. Dupont Summer Theater. Wynton Marsalis, Betty Carter, and Ramsey Lewis are among the artists who have performed free concerts. ✉ *Minnesota Ave. and Randall Circle SE,* ☎ *202/426–7723 or 202/619–7222.*

Sylvan Theater. Military bands from all four branches perform alfresco at the Sylvan Theater from June to August, Tuesday, Friday, and Sunday nights at 8 PM. ✉ *Washington Monument grounds,* ☎ *202/619–7222.*

Transparent Productions. Composed of a small group of dedicated jazz connoisseurs, this not-for-profit presenting organization regularly brings acclaimed avant-garde jazz musicians to intimate clubs and university stages. Past performers have included guitarist Joe Morris, bassist William Parker, and saxophonist Anthony Braxton. Tickets are usually in the $10 range, with 100% of the revenues going directly to the artists. ☎ *202/232–5061.*

Theater and Performance Art

Commercial Theaters

Arena Stage. The city's most respected resident company (established in 1950) was also the first outside New York to win a Tony award. It presents a wide-ranging season in its three theaters: the Fichandler Stage, the proscenium Kreeger, and the cabaret-style Old Vat Room. ⊠ *6th St. and Maine Ave. SW,* ☎ *202/488–3300.*

Ford's Theatre. Looking much as it did when President Lincoln was shot at a performance of *Our American Cousin,* Ford's hosts both dramas and musicals, many with family appeal. ⊠ *511 10th St. NW,* ☎ *202/347–4833.*

Lincoln Theatre. From the 1920s to the 1940s, the Lincoln hosted the same performers as the Cotton Club and the Apollo Theatre in New York City: Cab Calloway, Lena Horne, Duke Ellington. The 1,250-seater shows films and welcomes such acts as the Count Basie Orchestra and the Harlem Boys and Girls Choir. ⊠ *1215 U St. NW,* ☎ *202/ 328–6000.*

National Theatre. Destroyed by fire and rebuilt four times, the National Theatre has operated in the same location since 1835. It presents touring Broadway shows and offers free children's shows on Saturday. Winter and spring see a series of free Monday-night shows that run the gamut from Asian dance to performance art to a cappella cabarets. ⊠ *1321 Pennsylvania Ave. NW,* ☎ *202/628–6161.*

Shakespeare Theatre. Four plays—three by the Bard, another a classic from his era—are staged each year by the acclaimed Shakespeare Theatre troupe in a state-of-the-art, 450-seat space. ⊠ *450 7th St. NW,* ☎ *202/393–2700.*

Warner Theatre. One of Washington's grand theaters, this 1924 building hosts road shows, dance recitals, pop music, and the occasional comedy act. ⊠ *13th and E Sts. NW,* ☎ *202/783–4000.*

Small Theaters and Companies

Gala Hispanic Theatre. The company produces Spanish classics as well as contemporary and modern Latin American plays in both Spanish and English. ⊠ *1625 Park Rd. NW,* ☎ *202/234–7174.*

Source Theatre. The 107-seat Source Theatre presents established plays with a sharp satirical edge and modern interpretations of classics. Each summer, Source hosts the Washington Theater Festival, a series of new plays, many by local playwrights. ⊠ *1835 14th St. NW,* ☎ *202/462–1073.*

Studio Theatre. This small, independent company has an eclectic season of classic and offbeat plays. With two 200-seat theaters, the Mead and the Milton, as well as the 50-seat Secondstage (home to particularly experimental works), the Studio Theatre is one of the busiest groups in the city. ⊠ *1333 P St. NW,* ☎ *202/332–3300.*

Washington Stage Guild. Washington Stage Guild performs the classics as well as more contemporary works in historic Carroll Hall. Shaw is a specialty. ⊠ *924 G St. NW,* ☎ *202/529–2084.*

Woolly Mammoth. Unusual, imaginatively produced shows have earned Woolly Mammoth good reviews and favorable comparisons to Chicago's Steppenwolf. ⊠ *1401 Church St. NW,* ☎ *202/393–3939.*

NIGHTLIFE

Washington's nightlife includes watering holes, comedy clubs, discos, and intimate musical venues that cater to a variety of customers—from proper political appointees to blue-collar regulars in from the 'burbs. Many places are clustered in key areas, making a night of bar-hopping relatively easy. Georgetown has dozens of bars, nightclubs, and restaurants on M Street east and west of Wisconsin Avenue and on Wisconsin Avenue north of M Street. Along the 18th Street strip in Adams-Morgan, bordered by Columbia Road and Florida Avenue, you'll find several small live music clubs, ethnic restaurants, and bars. West of Florida Avenue, the U Street corridor—considered by many to be one of the hippest neighborhoods in the country—appeals to twentysomethings looking for musical entertainment. On a stretch of

Pennsylvania Avenue between 2nd and 4th streets, you'll find a half dozen Capitol Hill bars. For a happenin' happy hour, head to the intersection of 19th and M streets NW, which is near the lawyer- and lobbyist-filled downtown.

To check out the local scene, consult Friday's "Weekend" section in the *Washington Post* and the free weekly *Washington CityPaper*. The free *Metro Weekly* and *Women in the Life* magazines offer insights on gay and lesbian nightlife. It's also a good idea to call clubs ahead of time to find out what's on. Reservations are advised for comedy clubs; places where reservations are essential are noted below.

Acoustic/Folk/Country Clubs

For information on folk events—from *contra* (a form of folk) dancing to storytelling—call the recorded information line of the **Folklore Society of Greater Washington** (☎ 202/546–2228).

Birchmere. Birchmere is one of the best places this side of the Blue Ridge Mountains to hear acoustic folk and bluegrass acts. Audiences come to listen, and the management politely insists on no distracting chatter. ⊠ *3701 Mt. Vernon Ave., Alexandria, VA,* ☎ *703/549–7500.* ☉ *Sun.–Thurs. 6:30 PM–11 PM, Fri.–Sat. 7 PM–12:30 AM.*

Food for Thought. Lots of Birkenstock sandals, natural fibers, and activist conversation give this Dupont Circle lounge-restaurant a '60s coffeehouse feel. Nightly folk music completes the picture. ⊠ *1738 Connecticut Ave. NW,* ☎ *202/797–1095.* ☉ *Mon. 11:30–3 and 5–12:30 AM, Tues.–Thurs. 11:30 AM–12:30 AM, Fri. 11:30 AM–1:30 AM, Sat. 12:30 PM–1:30 AM, Sun. 4 PM–12:30 AM.*

Bars and Lounges

Brickskeller. This is *the* place to go when you want something more exotic than a Bud Lite. More than 800 brands of beer are for sale—from Central American lagers to U.S. microbrewed ales. ⊠ *1523 22nd St. NW,* ☎ *202/293–1885.* ☉ *Mon.–Thurs. 11:30 AM–2 AM, Fri. 11:30 AM–3 AM, Sat. 6 PM–3 AM, Sun. 6 PM–2 AM.*

Capital City Brewing Company. In the New York Avenue location of this microbrewery, a gleaming copper bar dominates the airy room; metal steps lead up to where the brews—from bitters to bocks—are made. The fabulous Postal Square site on Massachusetts Avenue has five 30-keg copper serving vessels in the center of the restaurant. ⊠ *1100 New York Ave. NW,* ☎ *202/628–2222;* ⊠ *2 Massachusetts Ave. NE,* ☎ *202/842–2337.* ⊙ *Mon.–Sat. 11 AM–2 AM, Sun. 11 AM–midnight.*

Champions. Walls covered with jerseys, pucks, bats, and balls, and the evening's big game on the big-screen TV—this popular Georgetown establishment is a sports lover's oasis. ⊠ *1206 Wisconsin Ave. NW,* ☎ *202/965–4005.* ⊙ *Mon.–Thurs. 5 PM–2 AM, Fri. 5 PM–3 AM, Sat. 11:30 AM–3 AM, Sun. 11:30 AM–2 AM. 1-drink minimum Fri.–Sat. after 11 PM.*

Chi Cha Lounge. Groups of stylish twentysomethings relax on sofas and armchairs—enjoying the bar's menu of Andean appetizers, homemade sangria, and cocktails—while ambient Latin jazz plays in the background. It gets packed on weekends, so come early to get a coveted sofa along the back wall, where it's easier to see—and be seen. ⊠ *1624 U St. NW,* ☎ *202/234–8400.* ⊙ *Sun.–Thurs. 5 PM–2 AM, Fri.–Sat. 5 PM–3 AM.*

Dubliner. Snug paneled rooms, thick Guinness, and nightly live entertainment make Washington's premier Irish pub popular among Capitol Hill staffers. ⊠ *520 N. Capitol St. NW,* ☎ *202/737–3773.* ⊙ *Sun.–Thurs. 11 AM–1:30 AM, Fri.–Sat. 11 AM–2:30 AM.*

Sign of the Whale. The best hamburger in town is available at the bar of this well-known post-preppie/neo-yuppie haven. ⊠ *1825 M St. NW,* ☎ *202/785–1110.* ⊙ *Sun.–Thurs. 11:30 AM–1:30 AM, Fri.–Sat. 11:30 AM–2:30 AM.*

Comedy Clubs

Capitol Steps. The musical political satire of the Capitol Steps, a group of current and former Hill staffers, is presented on Friday and Saturday at Chelsea's (☞ Dance Clubs, *below*). ☎ *202/298–8222 (Chelsea's) or 703/683–8330 (Capitol Steps).* ⊡ *Cover charge.* ⊙ *Fri. at 8 and Sat. at 7:30 most wks. Reservations essential.*

Garvin's Comedy Clubs. Garvin's, which pioneered the practice of organizing comedy nights in suburban hotels, is one of the oldest names in comedy in the DC area. ⊠ *Westpark Hotel, 8401 Westpark Dr., Tysons Corner, VA,* ☎ *202/872–8880.* 🎫 *Cover charge and 2-drink minimum.* ☉ *Fri. at 9, Sat. 8 and 10. Reservations essential.*

Gross National Product. After years of spoofing Republican administrations with such shows as *BushCapades* and *Man Without a Contra,* then aiming its barbs at the Democrats in *Clintoons,* the irreverent comedy troupe Gross National Product was most recently performing *Sex, Lies and Paulagate.* ☎ *202/783–7212 (GNP) for location and reservations.* 🎫 *Ticket charge.* ☉ *Sat. at 7:30.*

Improv. A heavyweight on the Washington comedy scene, the Improv is descended from the club that sparked the stand-up boomlet in New York City and across the country. Name headliners are common. ⊠ *1140 Connecticut Ave. NW,* ☎ *202/296–7008.* 🎫 *Cover charge and 2-item (not necessarily drinks) minimum.* ☉ *Sun. and Wed.–Thurs. at 8:30, Fri.–Sat. at 8:30 and 10:30.*

Dance Clubs

Chelsea's. At this elegant Georgetown club near the C&O Canal, the DJ's trot the globe. Depending on the night, the club pulses to the rhythms of Arabic, Latin, or Greek music. ⊠ *1055 Thomas Jefferson St. NW,* ☎ *202/298–8222.* 🎫 *Cover charge Wed.–Sat.* ☉ *Wed.–Thurs. and Sun. 9:30 PM– 2 AM, Fri.–Sat. 10:30 PM–4 AM.*

Ritz. This nightclub near the FBI building is popular with a professional crowd, though on Friday nights the club becomes "Decades" and caters to a mixed over-21 clientele. The Ritz has five rooms, with DJs spinning a different type of music. ⊠ *919 E St. NW,* ☎ *202/638–2582.* 🎫 *Cover charge.* ☉ *Wed. 10 PM–2:30 AM, Fri. 9 PM–4 AM, Sat. 9 PM–4 AM, Sun. 10:30 PM–2:30 AM.*

State of the Union. State draws a young, eclectic crowd dressed in the requisite wide-leg jeans of today's casually hip. Patrons here tend to be serious music fans who come to dance or hold down a spot at the bar while the city's best DJs spin a mix of house music, techno, hip-hop, trance, and classic R&B sounds. ⊠ *1357 U St. NW,* ☎ *202/588–*

8926. ☎ *Cover charge.* ⊙ *Mon.–Thurs. 5 PM–2 AM, Fri. 5 PM–3 AM, Sat. 6 PM–3 AM, Sun. 7 PM–3 AM.*

Zei. Pronounced "zee," this New York–style dance club in a former electric power substation draws an international crowd that includes everything from dark-suited "hiplomats" to affluent exchange students. The relentless thump of Euro-pop complements a design that includes a wall of television sets that peer down on the proceedings. ✉ *1415 Zei Alley NW (14th St. between H and I Sts. NW),* ☎ *202/842–2445.* ☎ *Cover charge.* ⊙ *Thurs. 10 PM–2 AM, Fri.–Sat. 10 PM–3 AM (call for occasional weeknight events).*

Gay and Lesbian Dance Clubs

The Circle Tavern. In the heart of Dupont Circle, this bar–dance club anchors the area's gay scene. If you want to know what's going on, the Circle should be your first stop. In warm weather, a mostly male crowd congregates on the outdoor terrace. ✉ *1629 Connecticut Ave. NW,* ☎ *202/462–5575.* ⊙ *Sun.–Thurs. 11 AM–2 AM, Fri.–Sat. 11 AM–2:45 AM.*

Hung Jury. You can count on the women at the Hung Jury to make the most of the dance floor, where you're just as likely to hear the innuendo-laden lyrics of rapper Lil' Kim as you are an upbeat Top 40 dance track. ✉ *1819 H St. NW,* ☎ *202/785–8181.* ☎ *Cover charge.* ⊙ *Fri. 9 PM–4 AM, Sat. 8 PM–4 AM.*

Tracks 2000. A gay club with a large contingent of straight regulars, this warehouse-district disco has one of the largest dance floors in town and stays open well into the wee hours. In a scene where clubs disappear seasonally, Tracks stands out for its longevity. ✉ *1111 1st St. SE,* ☎ *202/488–3320.* ⊙ *Thurs. 9 PM–4 AM, Fri. 9 PM–5 AM, Sat. 8 PM–6 AM, Sun. 4 PM–9:30 PM (tea dance) and 9:30 PM–4 AM.*

Jazz and Blues Clubs

Blues Alley. The restaurant turns out Creole cooking, while cooking on stage you'll find such nationally known performers as Nancy Wilson, Joshua Redman, and Stanley Turrentine. ✉ *Rear 1073 Wisconsin Ave. NW,* ☎ *202/ 337–4141.* ☎ *Cover charge and $7 food/drink minimum.* ⊙ *Sun.–Thurs. 6 PM–midnight, Fri.–Sat. 6 PM–2 AM. Shows at 8 and 10, plus occasional midnight shows Fri.–Sat.*

Café Lautrec. The prints of Lautrec's work, French food, and Continental atmosphere are almost enough to convince you you're on the Left Bank of the Seine rather than the right bank of the Potomac. Cool cats play straight-ahead jazz nightly, with tap-dancing fixture Johne Forges hoofing atop tables most Fridays and Saturdays. ✉ *2431 18th St. NW,* ☎ *202/265–6436.* 🎫 *$6 minimum.* ◷ *Sun.– Thurs. 5 PM–2 AM, Fri.–Sat. 5 PM–3 AM.*

City Blues Cafe. On weeknights you might encounter an acoustic duo or a feathery-voice jazz chanteuse, but on weekends hard-driving blues bands rule (arrive early to get a good table). ✉ *2651 Connecticut Ave. NW,* ☎ *202/232–2300.* ◷ *Sun.–Thurs. noon–2 AM, Fri.–Sat. noon–3 AM.*

Columbia Station. When it opened in 1997, this place quickly became a neighborhood favorite, with its good food and great live music. Amber lights illuminate the brass instrument–theme artwork that adorns the walls. The nightly shows usually consist of a quality local jazz band and sometimes blues. ✉ *2325 18th St. NW,* ☎ *202/462–6040.* ◷ *Sun.–Thurs. 11 AM–1:45 AM, Fri.–Sat. 11 AM–2:30 AM.*

One Step Down. Low-ceilinged, intimate, and boasting the best jazz jukebox in town, One Step Down books talented local artists and the occasional national act. The venue of choice for many New York jazz masters, the place is frayed and smoky, as a jazz club should be. Live music is presented Thursday–Monday. ✉ *2517 Pennsylvania Ave. NW,* ☎ *202/ 995–7140.* 🎫 *Cover charge.* ◷ *Mon.–Thurs. 10 AM–2 AM, Fri. 10 AM–3 AM, Sat. noon–3 AM, Sun. noon–2 AM.*

Rock, Pop, and Rhythm-and-Blues Clubs

Bayou. In Georgetown, underneath the Whitehurst Freeway, the Bayou is a Washington fixture that showcases first-time national acts on weeknights and local talent on weekends. Tickets are available at the door or through Ticketmaster. ✉ *3135 K St. NW,* ☎ *202/333–2897.* 🎫 *Cover charge.* ◷ *Generally daily 8 PM–2 AM.*

The Ballroom. As one of the largest venues for alternative and rock music in Washington (it holds 1,000 people), the Ballroom brings in such bands as David Bowie, the Fugees, and Jamiroquai. Depending on the act, tickets are available at Ticketmaster or the door. ⊠ *1015 Half St. SE,* ☎ *202/ 554–1500.* 🎫 *Cover charge.* ☉ *Hrs vary according to show but generally at 7* PM *nightly. Dance club 10* PM.

9:30 Club. The 9:30 is a trendy club that books an eclectic mix of local, national, and international artists (most of them fall into the alternative-music category—from Paula Cole and Fiona Apple to Ziggy Marley and Erykah Badu). Get tickets at the door or through ProTix. ⊠ *815 V St. NW,* ☎ *202/393–0930.* 🎫 *Cover charge.* ☉ *Hrs vary according to shows but generally Sun.–Thurs. 7:30* PM– *midnight, Fri.–Sat. 9* PM–*2* AM.

6 Shopping

AFRICAN MASKS LIKE THOSE inspiring Picasso; kitchenware as objets d'art; bargains on apparel by Christian Dior, Hugo Boss, and Burberrys; paisley scarves from India; American and European antiques; books of every description; handicrafts from almost two dozen Native American tribes; music boxes by the thousand; textiles by the score; fine leather goods—all this and more can be found in the nation's capital.

By
Deborah
Papier

Updated
by Holly
Bass

Many Washingtonians still mourn the closing of Woodward & Lothrop's, one of downtown's finer department stores (indeed, all such local leviathans have closed with the exception of Hecht's). Discriminating shoppers can find satisfaction at Filene's Basement or at an upscale mall on the city's outskirts. On a more optimistic note, many of the smaller one-of-a-kind shops have survived urban renewal, the number of designer boutiques is on the rise, and interesting specialty shops and minimalls can be found all over town. Store hours vary greatly, so it's best to call ahead. In general, Georgetown stores are open late and on Sunday; stores downtown that cater to office workers close at 6 PM and may not be open at all on weekends. Some stores extend their hours on Thursday. Sales tax is 6%, and major credit cards and traveler's checks are accepted virtually everywhere. We list the shops' nearest Metro stations, but some shops might be a 15- to 20-minute walk from the Metro; we do not list Metro stops for the few stores that have no Metro within walking distance.

Adams-Morgan

Specialty Stores

ANTIQUES AND COLLECTIBLES

Chenonceau Antiques. The mostly American 19th- and 20th-century pieces on this shop's two floors were selected by a buyer with an exquisite eye. Merchandise includes beautiful 19th-century paisley scarves and 1920s glass lamps. ⊠ 2314 18th St. NW, ☎ 202/667–1651. ⊘ Weekends. Metro: Woodley Park.

Uniform. The best of the vintage clothing and household accessories shops in the neighborhood, Uniform has 1940s women's suits, 1950s party dresses, 1960s Nehru-collar jackets and A-line coats, disco-era halter tops, and all sorts of other formerly ordinary stuff now prized as icons of one bygone era or another. You'll also find plate ware that brings to mind *The Jetsons,* lava lamps, pillbox hats, navy pea coats, and Lucite heels. ⊠ *2407 18th St. NW,* ☎ *202/ 483–4577. Metro: Woodley Park.*

BOOKS

Yawa. Featuring a large collection of African and African-American fiction and nonfiction, magazines, and children's books, Yawa also sells ethnic jewelry, crafts, and greeting cards. ⊠ *2206 18th St. NW,* ☎ *202/483–6805. Metro: Dupont Circle.*

CRAFTS AND GIFTS

Skynear and Company. The owners travel the world to find the unusual. Their journeys have been successful, as here you'll find an extravagant assortment of rich textiles, furniture, and home accessories—all for the art of living. ⊠ *2122 18th St. NW,* ☎ *202/797–7160. Metro: Dupont Circle.*

MEN'S AND WOMEN'S CLOTHING

Kobos. A rainbow of clothing and accessories imported from West Africa is for sale at Kobos. ⊠ *2444 18th St. NW,* ☎ *202/332–9580. Metro: Dupont Circle.*

MUSIC

DC CD. This upstart music store caters to the club crowd with its late hours and wide selection of indie releases, rock, hip-hop, alternative, and soul. The knowledgeable staff will often open packages, allowing customers to listen before they buy. ⊠ *2423 18th St. NW,* ☎ *202/588–1810. Metro: Woodley Park*

SHOES

Shake Your Booty. Trend-conscious Washingtonians used to travel to Manhattan's West Village for modish leather boots and platform shoes. Now they just come here. ⊠ *2335 18th St. NW,* ☎ *202/518–8205. Metro: Woodley Park.*

WOMEN'S CLOTHING

Khismet Wearable Art. Traditional garments from West Africa and original fashions designed by Millée Spears, who lived in Ghana, fill colorful Khismet. Spears uses ethnic-print fabrics to create garments that are suitable for both work and an evening out and will custom design if desired. ⊠ *1800 Belmont Rd. NW,* ☎ *202/234–7778. Metro: Dupont Circle.*

Capitol Hill/Eastern Market

Mall

Union Station. This delightful shopping enclave is resplendent with marble floors and gilded, vaulted ceilings. It's now both a working train station and a mall with three levels—one with food stands and a cinema multiplex—of stores and, appropriately, the **Great Train Store,** which sells train memorabilia and toy versions from the inexpensive to four-digit Swiss models. The east hall, reminiscent of London's Covent Garden, is filled with vendors of expensive and ethnic wares in open stalls. Christmas is an especially pleasant time to shop here. ⊠ *Massachusetts Ave. NE near N. Capitol St.,* ☎ *202/371–9441. Metro: Union Station.*

Specialty Stores

BOOKS

Bird-in-Hand Bookstore & Gallery. This store specializes in books on art and design and also carries exhibition catalogs. ⊠ *323 7th St. SE,* ☎ *202/543–0744. Metro: Eastern Market.*

Trover Books. The latest political volumes and out-of-town newspapers are here. ⊠ *221 Pennsylvania Ave. SE,* ☎ *202/547–2665. Metro: Capitol South.*

CRAFTS AND GIFTS

Appalachian Spring. Appalachian Spring's two Washington stores sell traditional and contemporary American-made crafts, including quilts, jewelry, weavings, pottery, and blown glass. ⊠ *Union Station,* ☎ *202/682–0505. Metro: Union Station.*

Downtown

Department Stores

Filene's Basement. At this mecca for bargain hunters, you'll find steep discounts on Christian Dior, Hugo Boss, Burberrys, and other designer men's and women's labels. Off-price shoes, perfume, and accessories are sold as well. The downtown Filene's is especially well appointed in wood and brass; a handsome elevator takes you to the upper level. ⌧ *1133 Connecticut Ave. NW,* ☎ *202/872–8430. Metro: Farragut North.*

Hecht's. Bright and spacious, its sensible groupings and attractive displays of merchandise make shopping easy on the feet and the eyes. The clothes sold here are a mix of conservative and trendy lines, with the men's department assuming increasing importance. Cosmetics, lingerie, and housewares are also strong departments. Sadly, one of the things that makes Hecht's unique is that it's still open; all its downtown neighbors—Garfinckel's, Woodward & Lothrop, Lansburgh's—have pulled up stakes. As a clothing-department store it's roughly comparable to Macy's. ⌧ *12th and G Sts. NW,* ☎ *202/628–6661. Metro: Metro Center.*

Malls

Old Post Office Pavilion. The city is justly proud of its Old Post Office Pavilion, a handsome shopping center in a historic 19th-century building. In addition to a dozen food vendors, there are 17 shops. The observation deck in the building's clock tower has an excellent view of the city. ⌧ *1100 Pennsylvania Ave.,* ☎ *202/289–4224. Metro: Federal Triangle.*

Shops at National Place. The Shops takes up three levels, one of which is devoted to food stands. Although the stores are mainly youth-oriented (this is a good place to drop off teenagers weary of the Smithsonian and more in the mood to buy T-shirts), **Perfumania** and clothing stores such as **Oaktree** and **August Max** have branches here, too. ⌧ *13th and F Sts. NW,* ☎ *202/783–9090. Metro: Metro Center.*

Specialty Stores

BOOKS

Chapters. A "literary bookstore," Chapters eschews cartoon collections and diet guides, filling its shelves instead with serious contemporary fiction, classics, and poetry. ⌧ *1512 K St. NW,* ☎ *202/347–5495. Metro: Farragut North.*

CRAFTS AND GIFTS

Fahrney's. It started out as a pen bar—a place to fill your fountain pen before embarking on the day's business. Today, Fahrney's sells pens in silver, gold, and lacquer by the world's leading manufacturers. ⊠ *1430 G St. NW,* ☎ *202/628–9525. Metro: McPherson Square.*

Indian Craft Shop. Handicrafts, such as jewelry, pottery, sand paintings, weavings, and baskets from almost two dozen Native American tribes are for sale. Items range from inexpensive (as little as $6) jewelry on up to collector-quality antiques. ⊠ *Dept. of Interior, 1849 C St. NW, Room 1023,* ☎ *202/208–4056. Metro: Farragut West.*

Music Box Center. An exquisite specialty store, the Music Box Center provides listening opportunities via more than 1,500 music boxes that play a total of 500 melodies. ⊠ *918 F St. NW,* ☎ *202/783–9399. Metro: Gallery Place/ Chinatown.*

JEWELRY

Pampillonia Jewelers. Traditional designs in 18-karat gold and platinum are found here, including many pieces for men. ⊠ *1213 Connecticut Ave. NW,* ☎ *202/628–6305. Metro: Farragut North.*

Tiny Jewel Box. Here you'll find well-chosen estate jewelry, contemporary jewelry, and unique gifts. ⊠ *1147 Connecticut Ave. NW,* ☎ *202/393–2747. Metro: Farragut North.*

MEN'S AND WOMEN'S CLOTHING

Britches of Georgetown. The larger of the two Washington branches, this store has a wide selection of traditional but trend-conscious men's clothing. ⊠ *1776 K St. NW,* ☎ *202/347–8994. Metro: Farragut North.*

Brooks Brothers. The oldest men's store in America, Brooks Brothers has sold traditional formal and casual clothing since 1818. It is one of the largest men's specialty stores in the area and offers classic women's clothing as well. ⊠ *1840 L St. NW,* ☎ *202/659–4650. Metro: Farragut North.*

Burberrys. Burberrys made its reputation with the trench coat, but this British company also manufactures traditional men's and women's apparel. ⊠ *1155 Connecticut Ave. NW,* ☎ *202/463–3000. Metro: Farragut North.*

J. Press. J. Press was founded in 1902 as a custom shop for Yale University. It is a resolutely traditional clothier: Shetland and Irish wool sport coats are a specialty. ⊠ *1801 L St. NW,* ☎ *202/857–0120. Metro: Farragut North.*

MUSIC

Serenade Record Shop. This shop is especially strong in classical music. ⊠ *1800 M St. NW,* ☎ *202/452–0075. Metro: Farragut North.*

Tower Records. The 16,000-square-ft Tower Records offers Washington's best selection of music in all categories, plus videos and laser discs. ⊠ *2000 Pennsylvania Ave. NW,* ☎ *202/331–2400. Metro: Foggy Bottom.*

SHOES

Church's. Church's is an English company whose handmade men's shoes are noted for their comfort and durability. ⊠ *1820 L St. NW,* ☎ *202/296–3366. Metro: Farragut North.*

WOMEN'S CLOTHING

Ann Taylor. Ann Taylor sells sophisticated, trend-conscious fashions for women and has an excellent shoe department. In addition to its downtown store, other locations include Mazza Gallerie (☎ 202/244–1940), Georgetown (☎ 202/ 338–5290) and Union Station (☎ 202/371–8010). ⊠ *1720 K St. NW,* ☎ *202/466–3544. Metro: Farragut West.*

Betsy Fisher. Stylish is the word that best describes Betsy Fisher's clothing—a contemporary look for women of all ages. ⊠ *1224 Connecticut Ave. NW,* ☎ *202/785–1975. Metro: Farragut North.*

Chanel Boutique. The Willard Hotel annex is where to find goodies from this legendary house of fashion. ⊠ *1455 Pennsylvania Ave. NW,* ☎ *202/638–5055. Metro: Metro Center.*

Rizik Bros. Rizik Bros. is a Washington institution combining designer clothing and accessories with expert service. The sales staff is trained to find just the right style from the large inventory, and prices are right. Take the elevator up from the northwest corner of Connecticut and L streets. ⊠ *1100 Connecticut Ave. NW,* ☎ *202/223–4050. Metro: Farragut North.*

Dupont Circle

Specialty Stores

ANTIQUES AND COLLECTIBLES

Cherishables. American 18th- and 19th-century furniture and decorative arts are the featured attractions here. Handmade, original Christmas ornaments are available year-round. ⊠ *1608 20th St. NW,* ☎ *202/785–4087. Metro: Dupont Circle.*

Marston Luce. Focusing on American folk art, including quilts, weather vanes, and hooked rugs, Marston Luce also carries home and garden furnishings, primarily American, but some English and French as well. ⊠ *1314 21st St. NW,* ☎ *202/775–9460. Metro: Dupont Circle.*

BOOKS

Kramerbooks. Open 24 hours on weekends, Kramerbooks shares space with a café that has late-night dining and weekend entertainment. The stock is small but well selected. ⊠ *1517 Connecticut Ave. NW,* ☎ *202/387–1400. Metro: Dupont Circle.*

Lammas Books. A selection of music by women as well as women's and lesbian literature is for sale here. Customers can connect with like minds via the store's public Internet-ready computer. ⊠ *1607 17th St. NW,* ☎ *202/775–8218. Metro: Dupont Circle.*

Second Story Books. A mecca for bibliophiles that encourages hours of browsing, this used-books and -records emporium stays open late. ⊠ *2000 P St. NW,* ☎ *202/659–8884. Metro: Dupont Circle.*

Vertigo Books. Just south of Dupont Circle, Vertigo Books emphasizes international politics, world literature, and African-American studies and presents an impressive series of regular author readings. ⊠ *1337 Connecticut Ave. NW,* ☎ *202/429–9272. Metro: Dupont Circle.*

CRAFTS AND GIFTS

Beadazzled. Head to Beadazzled for a truly dazzling array of ready-to-string beads and jewelry and books on crafts history and techniques. ⊠ *1507 Connecticut Ave. NW,* ☎ *202/265–2323. Metro: Dupont Circle.*

SHOES

Shoe Scene. The fashionable, moderately priced shoes for women found here are direct imports from Europe. ✉ *1330 Connecticut Ave. NW,* ☎ *202/659–2194. Metro: Dupont Circle.*

Georgetown

Mall

Shops at Georgetown Park. Near the hub of the Georgetown shopping district, at the intersection of Wisconsin Avenue and M Street, is this trilevel mall, which looks like a Victorian ice cream parlor inside. The pricey clothing and accessory boutiques and ubiquitous chain stores (such as Victoria's Secret) in this posh place draw international visitors in droves. Next door is a branch of **Dean & Deluca** (✉ 3276 M St. NW ☎ 202/342–2500), New York's premier gourmet food store. ✉ *3222 M St. NW,* ☎ *202/298–5577. Metro: Foggy Bottom.*

Specialty Stores

ANTIQUES AND COLLECTIBLES

Georgetown Antiques Center. The center, in a Victorian town house, has two dealers who share space: **Cherub Gallery** (☎ 202/337–2224) specializes in Art Nouveau and Art Deco, and **Michael Getz Antiques** (☎ 202/338–3811) sells fireplace equipment and silverware. ✉ *2918 M St. NW. Metro: Foggy Bottom.*

Miller & Arney Antiques. English, American, and European furniture and accessories from the 17th and early 19th centuries give Miller & Arney Antiques a museum-gallery air. Asian porcelain adds splashes of color. ✉ *1737 Wisconsin Ave. NW,* ☎ *202/338–2369. Metro: Foggy Bottom.*

Old Print Gallery. The capital's largest collection of old prints and maps (including Washingtoniana) is housed in this gallery. ✉ *1220 31st St. NW,* ☎ *202/965–1818. Metro: Foggy Bottom.*

Susquehanna. With three rooms upstairs, four rooms downstairs, and a garden full of cast-iron birdbaths, Susquehanna is the largest antiques shop in Georgetown. Paintings cover every inch of wall space, though the shop really specializes in American and English furniture. ✉ *3216 O St. NW,* ☎ *202/333–1511. Metro: Foggy Bottom.*

CRAFTS AND GIFTS

American Hand. This is a wonderful place for one-of-a-kind functional and nonfunctional pieces—tea kettles, corkscrews, glassware, and jewelry—by international designers. ✉ *2906 M St. NW,* ☎ *202/965–3273. Metro: Foggy Bottom.*

Appalachian Spring. The largest of this chain's four outlets (there are two suburban shops and another one on the Hill), Appalachian Spring has a wide selection of traditional and contemporary American-made crafts: quilts, jewelry, weavings, pottery, and blown glass. ✉ *1415 Wisconsin Ave. NW,* ☎ *202/337–5780.*

Phoenix. The Phoenix sells contemporary clothing in natural fibers by designers such as Aileen Fisher and Flax, as well as jewelry and art pieces (fine and folk) from Mexico. ✉ *1514 Wisconsin Ave. NW,* ☎ *202/338–4404.*

KITCHENWARE

Little Caledonia. Little Caledonia has nine rooms crammed with thousands of unusual and imported items for the home. Candles, cards, fabrics, and lamps round out the stock of decorative kitchenware. ✉ *1419 Wisconsin Ave. NW,* ☎ *202/333–4700.*

LEATHER GOODS

Coach Store. For fine leather, the Coach Store carries a complete (and expensive) line of well-made handbags, briefcases, belts, and wallets. ✉ *1214 Wisconsin Ave. NW,* ☎ *202/342–1772. Metro: Foggy Bottom.*

MEN'S AND WOMEN'S CLOTHING

Britches Great Outdoors. The casual version of Britches of Georgetown, Britches Great Outdoors has filled many Washington closets with rugby shirts and other sportswear. ✉ *1225 Wisconsin Ave. NW,* ☎ *202/333–3666. Metro: Foggy Bottom.*

Britches of Georgetown. Britches carries an extensive selection of traditional but trend-conscious designs in natural fibers for men. ✉ *1247 Wisconsin Ave. NW,* ☎ *202/338–3330. Metro: Foggy Bottom.*

Commander Salamander. This funky outpost sells trendy clothes for the alternative set—punk kids and ravers. Sifting through the assortment of leather, chains, toys, and candy-color makeup is as much entertainment as it is shopping. The store is open till 10 PM on weekends. ⊠ *1420 Wisconsin Ave. NW,* ☎ *202/337–2265. Metro: Foggy Bottom.*

MUSIC

musicnow. Here you'll find the latest electronic dance music in vinyl and CD formats. DJs often spin records in the house. If the music makes you feel like dancing, the shop also sells club-inspired clothing and has flyers advertising the week's raves. ⊠ *3209 M St. NW,* ☎ *202/338–5638. Metro: Foggy Bottom.*

Orpheus Records. Orpheus specializes in new and used jazz, rock, and blues records. There's also a small, well-chosen selection of new and used CDs and tapes. ⊠ *3249 M St. NW,* ☎ *202/337–7970.*

SHOES

Bootlegger. Chunky platforms, Birkenstocks sandals, black boots by NaNa, and Doc Marten's in all colors are staples at this retailer. ⊠ *1420 Wisconsin Ave. NW,* ☎ *202/333–0373. Metro: Foggy Bottom.*

WOMEN'S CLOTHING

Betsey Johnson. This shop sells fanciful frocks for the young and restless. ⊠ *1319 Wisconsin Ave. NW,* ☎ *202/338–4090. Metro: Foggy Bottom.*

Earl Allen. Earl Allen offers conservative but distinctive dresses and sportswear, wearable art, and one-of-a-kind items, much of it made exclusively for this small chain. ⊠ *3109 M St. NW,* ☎ *202/338–1678. Metro: Foggy Bottom.*

U Street

BOOKS

Sisterspace and Books. Sisterspace specializes in books written by and appealing to African-American women. In addition to selling books by authors such as Iyanla Vanzant, Maya Angelou, and Toni Morrison, the store offers seminars on everything from money and health to spirituality and creative fulfillment. ⊠ *1515 U St. NW,* ☎ *202/986–7092. Metro: U Street.*

MEN'S AND WOMEN'S CLOTHING

Mood Indigo. This vintage clothing store once had a 1940s theme, but now it has expanded to include suits, dresses, and hats and accessories from the '50s through the '70s. ⌧ *1214 U St. NW,* ☎ *202/256–6366. Metro: U Street.*

Trade Secrets. The textured wool, velvet, and silk designs in African-inspired patterns sold here seem almost too pretty to wear. Almost. ⌧ *1214 U St. NW,* ☎ *202/256–6366. Metro: U Street.*

Wisconsin Avenue

Department Stores

Filene's Basement. To really appreciate the bargains here, do some window shopping in Mazza Gallerie before entering this store from the mall. In addition to big savings on men's and women's clothing by well-regarded designers such as Hugo Boss and Christian Dior, Filene's has discounts on shoes, perfume, and accessories. ⌧ *5300 Wisconsin Ave. NW,* ☎ *202/966–0208. Metro: Friendship Heights.*

Lord & Taylor. Lord & Taylor lets the competition be all things to all people while it focuses on classic men's, women's, and children's clothing by such designers as Anne Klein and Ralph Lauren. ⌧ *5255 Western Ave. NW,* ☎ *202/362–9600. Metro: Friendship Heights.*

Neiman Marcus. If price is an object, this is definitely not the place to shop, although it's still a fun place to browse. Neiman Marcus caters to customers who value quality above all. The carefully selected merchandise includes couture clothes, furs, precious jewelry, crystal, and silver. ⌧ *Mazza Gallerie, 5300 Wisconsin Ave. NW,* ☎ *202/966–9700. Metro: Friendship Heights.*

Saks Fifth Avenue. Though not technically a Washington department store because it is just over the Maryland line, Saks is nonetheless a Washington institution. It has a wide selection of European and American couture clothes. ⌧ *5555 Wisconsin Ave.,* ☎ *301/657–9000. Metro: Friendship Heights.*

Malls

Chevy Chase Pavilion. Across from Mazza Gallerie (☞ *below*) is the newer, similarly upscale Chevy Chase Pavilion. Its exclusive women's clothing stores include **Joan & David** and **Steilmann European Selection** (which carries Karl Lagerfeld's sportier KL line). Other specialty shops of note here are **Pottery Barn** and **Country Road Australia.** ⊠ *5335 Wisconsin Ave. NW,* ☎ *202/686–5335. Metro: Friendship Heights.*

Mazza Gallerie. The four-level Mazza Gallerie is anchored by the ritzy **Neiman Marcus** department store and the discount department store **Filene's Basement.** Other stores include **Williams-Sonoma's** kitchenware and **Laura Ashley Home** as well as branches of **Skynear, Pampillonia Jewelers,** and **Ann Taylor.** ⊠ *5300 Wisconsin Ave. NW,* ☎ *202/ 966–6114. Metro: Friendship Heights.*

Specialty Stores

BOOKS

Travel Books & Language. One of the largest specialty bookshops of its kind in the country, Travel Books & Language has an enormous stock of travel guides, cookbooks, travel narratives, maps, and language-study workbooks and audio tapes. ⊠ *4437 Wisconsin Ave. NW,* ☎ *202/237– 1322. Metro: Tenleytown/American University.*

JEWELRY

Charles Schwartz & Son. A full-service jeweler, Charles Schwartz specializes in precious stones in traditional and modern settings. Fine watches are also offered. ⊠ *Mazza Gallerie, 5300 Wisconsin Ave. NW,* ☎ *202/363–5432. Metro: Friendship Heights.*

INDEX

NOTES

NOTES

NOTES

NOTES

NOTES

NOTES

NOTES

NOTES

NOTES

Looking for a different kind of vacation?

Fodor's makes it easy with a full line of specialty guidebooks to suit a variety of interests—from sports and adventure to romance to family fun.

At bookstores everywhere.
www.fodors.com

Fodor's Travel Publications

Available at bookstores everywhere. For descriptions of all our titles and a key to Fodor's guidebook series, visit www.fodors.com/books

Gold Guides
U.S.

Alaska
Arizona
Boston
California
Cape Cod, Martha's Vineyard, Nantucket
The Carolinas & Georgia
Chicago
Colorado

Florida
Hawai'i
Las Vegas, Reno, Tahoe
Los Angeles
Maine, Vermont, New Hampshire
Maui & Lāna'i
Miami & the Keys
New England
New Orleans

New York City
Oregon
Pacific North Coast
Philadelphia & the Pennsylvania Dutch Country
The Rockies
San Diego
San Francisco

Santa Fe, Taos, Albuquerque
Seattle & Vancouver
The South
U.S. & British Virgin Islands
USA
Virginia & Maryland
Washington, D.C.

Foreign

Australia
Austria
The Bahamas
Belize & Guatemala
Bermuda
Canada
Cancún, Cozumel, Yucatán Peninsula
Caribbean
China
Costa Rica
Cuba
The Czech Republic & Slovakia
Denmark

Eastern & Central Europe
Europe
Florence, Tuscany & Umbria
France
Germany
Great Britain
Greece
Hong Kong
India
Ireland
Israel
Italy
Japan
London

Madrid & Barcelona
Mexico
Montréal & Québec City
Moscow, St. Petersburg, Kiev
The Netherlands, Belgium & Luxembourg
New Zealand
Norway
Nova Scotia, New Brunswick, Prince Edward Island
Paris
Portugal

Provence & the Riviera
Scandinavia
Scotland
Singapore
South Africa
South America
Southeast Asia
Spain
Sweden
Switzerland
Thailand
Toronto
Turkey
Vienna & the Danube Valley
Vietnam

Special-Interest Guides

Adventures to Imagine
Alaska Ports of Call
Ballpark Vacations
The Best Cruises
Caribbean Ports of Call
The Complete Guide to America's National Parks
Europe Ports of Call
Family Adventures
Fodor's Gay Guide to the USA

Fodor's How to Pack
Great American Learning Vacations
Great American Sports & Adventure Vacations
Great American Vacations
Great American Vacations for Travelers with Disabilities
Halliday's New Orleans Food Explorer

Healthy Escapes
Kodak Guide to Shooting Great Travel Pictures
National Parks and Seashores of the East
National Parks of the West
Nights to Imagine
Orlando Like a Pro
Rock & Roll Traveler Great Britain and Ireland

Rock & Roll Traveler USA
Sunday in San Francisco
Walt Disney World for Adults
Weekends in New York
Wendy Perrin's Secrets Every Smart Traveler Should Know
Worlds to Imagine

Fodor's Special Series

Fodor's Best Bed & Breakfasts
America
California
The Mid-Atlantic
New England
The Pacific Northwest
The South
The Southwest
The Upper Great
Lakes

Compass American Guides
Alaska
Arizona
Boston
Chicago
Coastal California
Colorado
Florida
Hawai'i
Hollywood
Idaho
Las Vegas
Maine
Manhattan
Minnesota
Montana
New Mexico
New Orleans
Oregon
Pacific Northwest
San Francisco
Santa Fe
South Carolina
South Dakota
Southwest
Texas
Underwater Wonders
of the National Parks
Utah
Virginia
Washington
Wine Country
Wisconsin
Wyoming

Citypacks
Amsterdam
Atlanta
Berlin
Boston
Chicago
Florence
Hong Kong
London
Los Angeles
Miami
Montréal
New York City
Paris
Prague
Rome

San Francisco
Sydney
Tokyo
Toronto
Venice
Washington, D.C.

Exploring Guides
Australia
Boston &
New England
Britain
California
Canada
Caribbean
China
Costa Rica
Cuba
Egypt
Florence & Tuscany
Florida
France
Germany
Greek Islands
Hawai'i
India
Ireland
Israel
Italy
Japan
London
Mexico
Moscow &
St. Petersburg
New York City
Paris
Portugal
Prague
Provence
Rome
San Francisco
Scotland
Singapore & Malaysia
South Africa
Spain
Thailand
Turkey
Venice
Vietnam

Flashmaps
Boston
New York
San Francisco
Washington, D.C.

Fodor's Cityguides
Boston
New York
San Francisco

Fodor's Gay Guides
Amsterdam
Los Angeles &
Southern California

New York City
Pacific Northwest
San Francisco and
the Bay Area
South Florida
USA

Karen Brown Guides
Austria
California
England B&Bs
England, Wales &
Scotland
France B&Bs
France Inns
Germany
Ireland
Italy B&Bs
Italy Inns
Portugal
Spain
Switzerland

Languages for Travelers (Cassette & Phrasebook)
French
German
Italian
Spanish

Mobil Travel Guides
America's Best
Hotels & Restaurants
Arizona
California and the
West
Florida
Great Lakes
Major Cities
Mid-Atlantic
Northeast
Northwest and
Great Plains
Southeast
Southern California
Southwest and
South Central

Pocket Guides
Acapulco
Aruba
Atlanta
Barbados
Beijing
Berlin
Budapest
Dublin
Honolulu
Jamaica
London
Mexico City
New York City
Paris

Prague
Puerto Rico
Rome
San Francisco
Savannah &
Charleston
Shanghai
Sydney
Washington, D.C.

Rivages Guides
Bed and Breakfasts of
Character and Charm
in France
Hotels and Country
Inns of Character and
Charm in France
Hotels and Country
Inns of Character and
Charm in Italy
Hotels of Character
and Charm in Paris
Hotels of Character
and Charm in Portugal
Hotels of Character
and Charm in Spain
Wines & Vineyards
of Character and
Charm in France

Short Escapes
Britain
France
Near New York City
New England

Fodor's Sports
Golf Digest's
Places to Play (USA)
Golf Digest's Places to
Play in the Southeast
Golf Digest's Places to
Play in the Southwest
Skiing USA
USA Today The
Complete Four Sport
Stadium Guide

Fodor's upCLOSE Guides
California
Europe
France
Great Britain
Ireland
Italy
London
Los Angeles
Mexico
New York City
Paris
San Francisco

WHEREVER YOU TRAVEL, HELP IS NEVER FAR AWAY.

From planning your trip to providing travel assistance along the way, American Express® Travel Service Offices are always there to help you do more.

Washington, D.C.

American Express Travel Service
1150 Connecticut Avenue N.W.
202/457-1300

American Express Travel Service
5300 Wisconsin Avenue N.W.
Garden Level
Mazza Gallery
202/362-4000

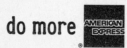

do more ® AMERICAN EXPRESS

Travel
www.americanexpress.com/travel

American Express Travel Service Offices
are located throughout the United States.
For the office nearest you, call 1-800-AXP-3429.

Listings are valid as of January 1999. Not all services available at all locations.
© 1999 American Express.